FACULTY BRAT

Winner of the
Iowa Prize
for Literary
Nonfiction

FACULTY
BRAT

A Memoir of Abuse

Dominic Bucca

UNIVERSITY OF IOWA PRESS, IOWA CITY

University of Iowa Press, Iowa City 52242
Copyright © 2020 by Dominic Bucca
www.uipress.uiowa.edu
Printed in the United States of America

Printed on acid-free paper

Library of Congress Cataloging-in-Publication Data
Names: Bucca, Dominic, 1978– author.
Title: Faculty brat: a memoir of abuse / Dominic Bucca.
Description: Iowa City: University of Iowa Press, 2020. |
"Winner of the Iowa prize for literary nonfiction."
Identifiers: LCCN 2019026582 (print) | LCCN 2019026583
(ebook) | ISBN 9781609386856 (paperback) |
ISBN 9781609386863 (ebook)
Subjects: LCSH: Bucca, Dominic, 1978– |
Sexually abused children—United States—Biography. |
Children of teachers—United States—Biography. |
Child sexual abuse—United States—Case studies.
Classification: LCC RJ507.S49 B86 2020 (print) | LCC RJ507.S49
(ebook) | DDC 618.92/858360092 [B]—dc23
LC record available at https://lccn.loc.gov/2019026582
LC ebook record available at https://lccn.loc.gov/2019026583

For Liam

Author's Note

The litigious nature of our era has necessarily led to a high degree of risk aversion. That the potential benefit of litigation is available almost exclusively to those privileged enough to afford it is central to the theme of this book. To protect myself and all those involved in publishing *Faculty Brat*, I have refrained from naming my stepfather or the schools at which he taught.

Names and/or particularly identifying characteristics of living individuals beyond my immediate family have been altered or omitted to protect their identities.

I

MARSHALL

The Once and Future Boy

ORIENTATION

IMAGINE YOU ARE the single mother of a toddler. You are in your midtwenties, recently graduated from college, alone in an unfamiliar part of the country, trying to make a living. You were adopted by older parents. Your mother died recently. Your father is ill. The father of your child, still your husband, is an alcoholic philanderer with a shocking lack of impulse control, unwilling to remain faithful to you. He has chosen to stay in Maryland while you move a significant distance away to pursue your teaching career. You get a job and begin building that career with some degree of success. You have a barely livable salary, a home provided by your employer, and your own car, even though your parents did not allow you to learn to drive until you were about to graduate from college and become a mother. You begin making a life for yourself and your son. Soon, you meet a man.

And what sort of man? Interesting, certainly. He is intelligent, well traveled and well read, talented, a musician. His voice is deep, mesmerizing, and he commands his classroom without equal. It is 1982. He has long hair like your child's father, but he dresses smartly, not like your child's father or most other lovers you had during that era. He wears navy blazers with brass buttons and pleated khakis to work. He is handsome, fit, preppy, perfectly suited to his English teaching position. He coaches soccer, and the boys he coaches adore him. He loves music you've never heard of, music from Africa, India, and South America. Not only does he love that music, he plays it professionally, for actual, if very little, money.

He begins telling you his family history. It is like nothing you've ever heard. Foreign, romantic, rich. There is a castle on the Hudson, a his-

3

tory of friends and associates with names like Rockefeller and Roosevelt and even Kennedy, and while the family doesn't have money the way it once did, his parents still live in the Hamptons. You are seduced by his pedigree and the idea of the life this man and his family can provide for you and your son. You will summer and weekend in the Hamptons. You set about getting a divorce from your restaurant-manager husband. In six months, you will marry this man.

Nearly thirty years will pass before you learn his true nature. Or so you will tell yourself.

Imagine you are this woman.

Now, remember your boy.

PRESCHOOL

IN 1981 THE BOY's mother secures her first real job. Before this offer, her work has been limited to waiting tables and selling art supplies. Now she will teach art and English at a boarding school for learning-disabled students. The school is located in upstate New York, four hundred miles from her son's birthplace and their current home in western Maryland. In addition to her $12,000 salary, the school will provide a small but private cottage on campus and even meals during the school year. Thrilled, his mother accepts.

The boy is three years old. His mother packs her newly acquired Honda Civic with clothes and immediate necessities. His father will follow with furniture and the rest of their belongings in a rented truck, then help move his wife and son into their new home before returning to Maryland.

The boy has heard the terms "separation" and "divorce" many times recently but has no real understanding of their meanings. He does understand that his mother has been sad for some time. Suddenly, she is happy.

Her happiness is contagious. The boy will never forget the particular blend of safety and adventure his mother conjures for him during those first summer weeks in their new home. His father is suddenly absent, and this is confusing, but his mother is newly full of life, and this is fun.

Despite his lack of understanding, the boy is content to participate in his mother's newfound joy. Before the school year begins, they spend their days adventuring together, touring their new surroundings on foot and in her little car. In the evenings, they eat pizza on the floor and sort through boxes of books and records, heirlooms and art supplies. They set up the turntable and listen to Harry Nilsson's children's rock opera, *The Point!*, over and over. They sing along, cross-legged on the floor, swaying and smiling and happy.

Summer soon ends, and his mother's job begins. Her days become full as only boarding school days can, much longer than the boy's own days spent at the local preschool. Her work day begins promptly at 7:30 a.m. and often lasts until after 9:00 p.m. She is allowed two weekends off each month. A similarly exhausted teacher recommends a flexible babysitter: Kathy.

The boy will spend much of each week in Kathy's care for the next five years. The boy will remember her as a stern, grey woman, always frowning, perpetually disappointed in him. His mother will insist that she was never anything but warm and kind. And to his mother, at least, she always was.

Kathy has a teenage son, Russell, whose primary love in life is his dirt bike. His rifle is a close second, and Russell has rigged a holster for it on the back of his bike, an ugly, poorly stitched leather contraption that he shows off at every opportunity with particular pride. After two years of countless afternoons and evenings spent at Kathy's house, Russell begins taking special interest in the boy.

Russell's interest is invariably unpleasant. It generally involves forcing one of his heavy catcher's mitts onto the boy's small hand and throwing baseballs at him that the boy has no hope of catching. Russell throws hard, and not, the boy will often reflect, just by five-year-old standards. Despite the bruises, the boy's mother seems pleased.

"Isn't that so nice that Russell plays with you," she gushes, as Kathy hands the boy off at the end of each long day while smiling her strictly-for-paying-parents smile. "In a few years, you'll be the star of the little leagues!"

Early one evening, while showing off his gun-toting dirt bike for the hundredth time, Russell coaxes the boy up onto its saddle. Before the boy can slide back off, Russell climbs on behind, engulfing the boy's hands in his as he grabs the handlebars. Russell fires up his bike, twisting the boy's wrists with his, immediately taking off into the nearby woods, popping a breath-stealing wheelie, whooping with frightening glee.

Resettling the bike and leaning close, Russell navigates a narrow trail, low-hanging pine branches whipping past, snagging at the boy's arms, his face, his eyes. Russell yells into the boy's ear, "I'm gonna teach you to shoot, big guy!" His breath smells like old bologna and American cheese, the meal Kathy served just after school.

Russell allows the bike to sputter to a stop in a nearby clearing. The ride lasted only moments, but the boy's legs feel loose, shaking in echo of the bike's gyrations, skinny sticks of Jell-O he is barely able to control. As he slides off the bike, his bare leg brushes against its hot carburetor. Even the sudden, searing pain is not enough to loosen his clamped teeth, muffling his startled shriek.

"Idiot," Russell mutters, kneeling to inspect the burn, a palm-sized red circle already blistering the boy's calf.

The burn will take weeks to heal. The boy won't remember how he ever explained it to his mother. But he will remember how much she hated it when he suddenly started using the word "idiot" at every opportunity.

Standing, Russell claps the boy on his back, nearly knocking him over. "You'll be fine, big guy. Come over here!"

The boy can barely keep his feet but dutifully complies. *My mother wouldn't like this,* he says to himself, over and over again, a mantra he never once utters aloud.

Russell has the boy stand just so, as if he's going to put the rifle in his hands. As the boy is finally gathering the will to force his mouth open in protest, Russell crouches behind him and levels the gun over his right shoulder, the trigger an inch or two from the boy's ear, and fires.

The gunshot compounds the terror of the bike ride. The boy is unable to hear, unable to think, completely overwhelmed by his ringing head. He experiences something that he'll think back on as a backhanded, unpleasant sort of meditation, his mind oddly blank, the fear so unimaginable that, all at once, it becomes unimagined.

Eventually, the boy will learn the name for that disturbing, oddly welcome sensation, an experience that will become intimately familiar in the years to come: dissociation.

In a way, he will always be grateful to Russell for the lesson.

SIMPLE MATH

HIS MOTHER MARRIES Stepfather twice. At four years old, the boy trusts the family joke that their union might be twice as strong as a result.

The first time, they're married in a small civil ceremony on a hillside somewhere on the grounds of the rural New York prep school where they teach, where they met. The school's administrators require nuptials before the couple will be allowed to live together on campus. The man who will forever alter the boy's trajectory had already been living in his mother's cottage through the summer, so they need to make it official before the start of the academic year, when the students return.

In the future, the boy will reflect that their marriage was twice as flawed as others and getting worse with each passing year. At least for him.

He will retain only snapshot memories of the first wedding. His mother stuffing him into an uncomfortable dark suit, tightening his tie against his throat. The beautiful day, sunny and hot. A few of his mother's and new Stepfather's closest friends present, but not their parents. The whole affair lasting too long for his liking. He will remember feeling hungry. He will have no recollection of the ceremony itself, only the photos that followed. In those photos, he is scowling.

FRACTIONS

HE HATES NAPTIME. In the early afternoon, Kathy herds the boy along with the rest of her charges onto thin blankets laid out on her living room's shag-carpeted floor. Six or eight children lying head to foot and side by side. She sits above them in an overstuffed easy chair, casually brandishing a flyswatter.

The slightest noise or movement, involuntary or not, results in a sudden, vicious swat. The boy earns at least one swat each afternoon. If his fidgeting persists, Kathy will exchange the flyswatter for a wooden spoon. Slowly, he is trained to stillness.

Years later, as a teenager, the boy will tell his mother about Russell, about naptime, about Kathy's flyswatters and wooden spoons, easier secrets to share than the one he'll keep buried deep until his thirties. When his mother expresses her horror, he'll allow that it may be difficult to distinguish wooden spoon bruises from the marks of rough play on little boys. He will make many allowances for his mother.

As he ages, it becomes easier to control his fidgets. Now seven years old, the boy feels certain that he's too old for naptime. But each afternoon, he obediently joins the other kids on the floor, eyes closed, never sleeping, forcing himself to vigilant stillness each time Kathy lashes out to swat one of the younger children.

The boy's newly learned vigilance follows him home, where his newly acquired Stepfather makes him nervous. Stepfather wants the boy to call him "Dad." The word feels foreign to his mouth, so unpracticed. But the boy complies, wanting to please, each time thinking, *but you're not my real Dad.*

Perhaps in an effort to talk himself into it, the boy begins telling

Stepfather that he loves him at every opportunity. They are the first and last words uttered by the boy each time he encounters Stepfather, "I love you, Dad!"

"Watch out for that," a visiting friend warns Stepfather.

"Why? Isn't it great? The boy loves me!" Stepfather replies.

The boy has a new sister, who fascinates him. He sits on the couch with her at every opportunity, cradling her in his lap, foregoing the rarity of playtime at home in favor of holding her chubby little body, quietly marveling at her curling feet and strong, grabby hands while feeding her formula.

"Dominic loves his sister so much!" his mother often exclaims, beaming.

"*Half* sister," Stepfather often corrects.

"I love you, Dad!" the boy asserts as Stepfather lifts his sister—his *half* sister—out of his lap.

Although they now live off campus, his mother and Stepfather continue to work at the school where they'd met and married. During the academic year, the new family is rarely together save for early in the morning and late at night. Kathy remains a daily part of the boy's life.

The boy becomes remarkably tall for his age. As he grows, Kathy seems to grow more impatient with him, often swatting at him with her flyswatter even when it isn't naptime, often for no reason the boy can discern. Then the overnights begin.

His newlywed parents, wanting time alone, begin occasionally leaving the boy and his year-old sister with Kathy through the night. Kathy dotes on his little sister. At bedtime, Kathy takes his sister to her own bed to sleep. Kathy sends the boy to the couch in the living room, the hated naptime room.

The first time he wets himself at Kathy's there is no plastic sheet down, and his urine soaks through the couch cushions. The boy wakes with the dawn to find himself sticky, damp, and cold. Unsure what to do, he lies perfectly still, marinating in his own urine until Kathy descends from her bedroom, carrying his sister. Noticing the smell, then his guilty face, Kathy hauls the boy off the couch by his arm, wrenching his shoulder, yelling incoherently, furious in a way he has never seen.

His sister begins to cry. The boy is scared to silence. He clutches his aching shoulder, waiting to be told what to do.

Kathy strips the boy naked one-handed, his sister still propped in her arm, and marches the boy out to the kitchen, commanding him to "Stand there and don't move!" The boy silently obeys, listening closely as Kathy furiously tears the couch and bedding apart, observing as she marches back and forth, a soaked couch cushion in one arm, his crying sister in the other, tossing the cushions, one by one, out the front door onto the porch beyond, looking directly at him on each pass. He averts his eyes, making a study of the orange stars and squares that pattern the kitchen linoleum. Unbelievably, he feels the need to pee.

Parents arrive to drop off their children for the day. Still, the boy stands in the kitchen, naked, silent, ashamed.

The boy will never forget the sensation of his eyes departing from his body, observing himself from a detached point somewhere slightly behind and above his painfully wrenched shoulder. He will never forget Russell, pointing and laughing at him that morning. He won't remember how many parents and children saw him standing there naked, and he won't remember whether anyone asked, "Hey, what's with the naked kid in your kitchen?"

He was too self-conscious to notice anything beyond Russell's ridicule and Kathy's fury, too cold, scared, too devastatingly embarrassed. Years will pass before he'll realize that, once again, he had dissociated.

Even when he tells his mother about Russell's gun and Kathy's flyswatters and wooden spoons, the boy will keep this incident to himself. He will remember overhearing some of a conversation between his mother and Kathy about his "accidents." He will remember his mother sounding apologetic. He will remember that, on subsequent overnights, the couch was covered with a plastic sheet. He will remember how his urine pooled in the valleys of plastic created by his lithe, young body every morning he woke up on that couch.

In his early teenage years, the boy will experience a recurring dream of being naked in public. In his dream, he might be in any sort of situation, among friends, having fun, and suddenly he'd be naked. The boy desperately tries to explain his nudity, but no one hears him. They just laugh and point and the boy invariably startles himself awake to find himself drenched in sweat and piss, even years after his chronic bed-wetting finally stopped.

Years later, it will occur to him that his accidents stopped around the same time that Stepfather stopped visiting his bedroom late at night.

And yet, the dream persisted.

STUDY HALL

IN 1986, HIS MOTHER and Stepfather secure jobs and housing at a more prestigious prep school in northwestern Connecticut. His sister is two and the boy is eight. Their new home is less than an hour away, but Litchfield County seems like a different country compared to Duchess County, New York; wealthier and somehow more serious, committed to perfection even in its crumbling stone walls and rambling colonial mansions.

Like all generational prep schools in the Northeast, this school has its own coat of arms, a brightly painted shield with a motto ribboned across it. The original hangs in the foyer of the school's main administration building. The building is older than America, the shield likely even older than the building, and the motto is older still, the words claimed from the Bible by some British forebearer.

As a child recently arrived in this citadel of education, this school at which he'll learn his most painful lessons, the boy stands under that shield at every opportunity, looking up, studying every crack in the paint, fantasizing about carrying it into some medieval battle while his mother proctors study hall in the nearby library. The words seem transcendentally powerful, like suddenly discovering meaning in a slightly foreign language, like Shakespeare to an eight year old.

It reads: "Ye shall know the truth, and the truth shall make you free."

FACULTY BRAT

THAT'S WHAT THEY call children of educators at boarding schools. Faculty brats. *They* are members of the second-tier prep school hierarchy in descending order of importance: the administrators, the teachers, the students, the maintenance and dining hall and janitorial staff.

They are headmasters of schools you've only heard of if you were rejected by the likes of Exeter or Hotchkiss, but they are paid salaries that can't be looked down on by anyone and housed in homes adjacent to local elites who only return home from their park-view apartments on the weekend.

They are academic deans comfortable in their current importance, perhaps slightly embarrassed that they never finished their PhDs but nevertheless confident in their new ambition to become headmasters. They are English teachers with slightly-too-long hair, dressed in worn khaki and tweed with patches at the elbows and badly scuffed penny loafers. Their ties are too short, too old, and loose at the neck, and their leather bag briefcases are falling to pieces. If they were students, they'd get daily demerits for dress code violations. Once, they *were* students, often at the same school where they now grudgingly teach for salaries that are eclipsed by the current tuition at their hallowed alma mater.

They are the students themselves, the vast majority children of unimaginable privilege orphaned by their executive fathers and lawyer-or-doctor-or-painter-or-model-turned-socialite mothers to the care of a system of education that predates the creation of the American public school by centuries, taking its cues not so much from current pedagogical ideals but from the traditions of British schools that date back to the era of active monarchies. When they are not in session, they are on perpetual vacation from both school and family, skiing at Stowe or Aspen in the winter, "backpacking" Europe or India with a black AmEx in the summer. They will dine with their parents a handful of times before graduation, when ownership of the obligatory trust fund will be at least partially doled out.

They are the staff, locals who instinctively hate the school and the oligarchy it represents but are grateful for a job that recognizes all the holidays and then some. If they are cruel, they will take advantage of tuition remission to send their own children to the school, subjecting them to four years of day-student-townie status among boarding peers with home addresses in Manhattan's Upper East Side or Midtown or abroad. These local kids will likely befriend the few scholarship students and suffer through, and when they graduate they will discover that their claim to a place within the halls of Harvard or Yale or Princeton is only slightly stronger than that of the public school peers they left behind.

And then there is him. The faculty brat. He is the ten-year-old boy constantly underfoot, taking advantage of every corner of the thousand-acre campus, the only privilege he is afforded. He is first to the gymnasium nearly every day, monopolizing one of the four basketball hoops or climbing the faux rock wall while avoiding the gaze of disapproving upperclassmen and the athletic director. He is in the pool whenever it's open, equally embarrassed and enthralled by the older girls reclining on chaise lounges all around its edges with their magazines and low conversation and what he's certain are snickers aimed in his direction. He is at the tennis courts beating found balls against the backboard with a found racquet because no one will play with him. He is on his mountain bike, a shabby K-Mart affair that gets exponentially more use than the sophisticated Specialized machines owned by the students, annoying the cross-country runners at their practice on the trails behind campus. He is at the dining hall minutes before every meal, angling for a sandwich or a salad or a dessert before all the good stuff is gone, maddening the staff to no end, not caring because they're staff and he already understands the hierarchy. With few exceptions, the boy is despised, but he must be tolerated.

DISTILLED

THE FIRST TIME he gets drunk is with Stepfather. The boy is barely ten years old. He can't quite remember specific instances of Stepfather's unwanted intimacy before that night of drinking, can't quite remember how or why or exactly when it began, but he knows it had happened before. He has some idea of what to expect.

The drink is Jack Daniels, the squat, square bottle offering a perfect handhold. The bottle's surface is slick with a slight sheen of condensation. The bottle isn't cold, exactly, but they're in the cellar and the night is hot. The label's edge calls to the boy, its corners ever so slightly upraised, just enough to curl as his fingernails work at it, his hand wrapped around the slight bulb in the neck just below the glass spiral from which the cheap screw cap came off.

The boy will remember the label itself, black against the brown liquor, becoming more defined as the bottle emptied. The words Tennessee Whiskey and Sour Mash in block white letters proudly proclaimed in lettering styled to denote an earlier age. He will remember the smell: sour, just as the label promised.

The boy dreads Stepfather's lectures even as his actions invite them. Tall for his age, lazy, and still growing, the boy has already met puberty. Yet he wets his bed every other night, reminding himself that he's still a child, and a flawed child at that. He can't be bothered by his studies, let alone the nightly chores, a Cinderella-like regimen of washing dishes, wiping down the kitchen with Fantastik, sweeping the floors, and taking out the trash. He shirks often, never without consequence.

The lectures begin with a series of questions, almost always in the kitchen, almost always well after dark.

"Why didn't you take out the trash?" Stepfather asks.

"I forgot," the boy answers.

"How could you forget?"

"I don't know."

From there the conversation circles and circles in ever-greater concentricity around the same recurring topics, Stepfather's frustration evolving into fury.

"Why do you treat me this way?" Stepfather demands.

"I don't know," the boy responds.

"Why don't you talk to me?" Stepfather asks.

"I don't know," he responds.

"Why don't you trust me?" Stepfather asks.

"I don't know," he says again, avoiding the ever-present, ultimately devastating answer to all the questions:

Because you're not my dad.

These question-and-answer sessions stretch late into the night, well after the boy's mother succumbs to frustrated exhaustion.

At some point, inevitably, Stepfather becomes euphoric, perceiving some breakthrough, generally the result of the boy's own careful manipulation. Eventually, he allows Stepfather beyond those stoic "I don't know" responses, not quite giving in but giving just enough. Perhaps there will be some crying, followed by some manly backslapping. The result is always the same. The tone shifts, becoming less a lecture and more a discussion between equals. From *What's wrong with you?* to *How are you and I going to figure this out?*

What are we going to do to fix this?

This particular night, the catalyst for the shift between lecture and discussion is the Jack Daniels. Stepfather pulls the bottle down from the cupboard during the more heated part of the lecture. Soon they end up in the cellar study, stretched out before the cold fireplace. Stepfather smokes Marlboros but hates the filters. Stepfather rips the filters off his cigarettes twice an hour all day long, with increased frequency when the boy requires discipline.

Stepfather pours the first shot of Jack Daniels, offering it with a smile. Then the boy pours for himself, becoming intimate with that square, squat bottle. He asks for cigarettes. Stepfather obliges his every wish. The boy rips the filters off, thinking that's just what's done. Loose strands of tobacco catch on his lips. The boy spits them into the ashtray, just like Stepfather. The boy becomes drunk on whiskey, heady with the adultness of puffing on cigarettes. He is invincible. He can fix anything.

That night, the boy lost time to the whiskey, but he will remember the bathtub. He will remember the smell of his own vomit, pooling in the tub around his feet, sour and sweet and simply awful. He will remember Stepfather's hands on his back and in his hair, Stepfather's voice murmuring to him, all recalled through the muddy haze of drunkenness.

The boy is naked, sitting in the empty tub, vomiting uncontrollably. The window lightens with dawn. The boy continues vomiting, over and over again. The boy's mother comes downstairs in the morning.

"He's sick," Stepfather explains.

His mother answers, "I can see that."

She helps the boy from the tub and puts him to bed, forcing him to drink glass after glass of water. So much water. He doesn't want it, but he drinks because his mother asks him to.

The boy will remember the complete, utter safety of that moment. His mother, caring for him, putting him to bed. He will stay in bed for the next two days. He will have no interaction with Stepfather. He will begin to feel better, basking in the uninterrupted ease of his mother's care.

The sensation of those few days of safety provided by his mother will stay with the boy for the rest of his life, a haunting marker for what could have—should have—been.

The night before the boy goes back to school, Stepfather visits his room. The boy will often wonder whether it was his newfound experience with drunkenness, with the muddiness that went along with it, that lent such clarity to the memory of that sober night. The days before, spent exclusively in his mother's care, made him feel so safe.

He was not.

Stepfather enters the boy's room, silently closing the door behind him. Stepfather sits on the bed. He reaches out for the boy's hand, which the boy limply offers. Stepfather tells the boy that he is sorry. He tells the boy that he loves him. Stepfather is only searching for ways to be closer to the boy. Stepfather speaks about how much he regrets the distance between them. Stepfather lies down on the bed, next to the boy.

Stepfather continues talking, but the boy doesn't hear his words. The boy is only aware of Stepfather's hand, reaching under the covers, stroking the boy's legs, eventually wrapping around the boy's penis. The boy is embarrassingly hard. He stifles a flinch as Stepfather's wrapped fingers pull at the wisps of the boy's first pubic hairs.

The boy is silent and perfectly still.

Stepfather begins working the boy's penis with his hand. Eventually, he slips under the covers and takes the boy in his mouth. He works furiously.

The boy will remember Stepfather's mustache, rough against his most sensitive skin. He will remember how horribly good it felt when he came in Stepfather's mouth, how difficult it was to maintain his silent stillness. The sounds Stepfather made as he swallowed. The complete, crushing shame of how the boy enjoyed it, knowing that this was so—completely—wrong. It was the boy's first orgasm, and he wanted to scream his denial.

He will remember Stepfather rising, throwing back the covers as he left the boy's bed, wordlessly leaving the boy to his silence.

Nearly thirty years later, the man this boy is to become will remain unable to abide the smell of Jack Daniels Sour Mash Tennessee Whiskey. He will never taste the stuff again, yet he will have perfect, awful recall of it.

It tastes sour. Like shame.

THE DARK IS RISING

THE FIRST TIME HE runs away, *they* turn out in force. The boy is barely twelve years old, after all. His height, having recently surpassed Stepfather's six feet, makes it easy to forget that he is still a child. Suddenly everyone remembers.

His parents' fellow teachers and even the staff are genuinely concerned for the boy's well-being. Their bosses, the school's administrators, are also concerned, but their concern is for the school and its standing, its perception by the local community and beyond, that collection of intimidating names attached to the school's precious endowment and buildings. "Optics" is the astonishingly accurate word that will come to represent such concerns in the future, although it wasn't known then. Still, the sentiment was the same. Best to wrap up this unfortunate situation as expeditiously and quietly as possible, before word can leak off campus. Once the current crisis has passed, we will discuss how to prevent any recurrence.

The students also turn out. Their enthusiasm exceeds that of the teachers, although it has little to do with the boy's well-being. It is excitement born of the simple, narcissistic, ultimately human imperative for a situation, new and potentially emergent, something slightly dangerous outside the routine, allowing an opportunity for participation but ultimately devoid of the potential for harm to the self.

Whatever their reasons, they're all looking for the boy, some two hundred bodies strong, calling his name and waving flashlights.

The boy has no idea that anyone is looking for him, although as the sun sets he finds it increasingly difficult to ignore the nagging worry over the certain consequences that await him at home. Because the truth is, he has no intention of running away. He hasn't run anywhere.

He is sitting in a makeshift tent fashioned from found tarps and a rough, military-green blanket supported by branches between his two favorite trees at the edge of campus, just beyond the outer reaches of the school's cross-country course. In fact, he is at most a twenty-minute walk from his bedroom, and that only because, in the words of the boy's own cross-country coach, it's upsy.

The sun sets, and he puffs on one of the ten cigarettes he's stolen from Stepfather's packs over the last month. He's drunk nearly the whole cardboard quart of orange juice he swiped from home because he can't stand the acrid taste of his stolen cigarettes without immediate refreshment. He doesn't particularly like smoking, has never inhaled the smoke properly, and so doesn't quite understand what all the fuss is about, but he's been puffing steadily for some time and perhaps has become a bit high and certainly a bit ill through osmosis. He smokes because he can. There is one cigarette left.

The fact that true dark has settled does not concern him—he's been coming to this spot in these woods in the middle of the night for months. The boy has often reflected that the only reason he is still alive and relatively sane is that his bedroom has a door to the outside left in place after remodeling it from the kitchen it used to be when he was still too small to consider how bad life might become.

Now he knows.

His anxiety is rooted in his having made the conscious decision to come out here in the afternoon, when he wouldn't be missed for hours, and stay. For how long? He doesn't know the answer to that any more than he knew how bad life could get, but he's had ten cigarettes and a quart of OJ to figure it out. Now he worries that his juice may not last through his final cigarette, making all that careful theft seem futile.

So the darkness doesn't matter in itself. In fact, it's why he likes it here, between his favorite trees, a pair of ancient oaks with a nearly as ancient vine trying to bind the trees together and strangle them both. He likes it because it's just far enough from the campus proper to be away while still officially on campus, providing the flimsy illusion of safety from Stepfather's punishment.

And it is quiet. The only sounds are the wind, peepers, and the occasional small animal that sounds enormous but somehow doesn't scare him. No background noise from the twenty freshmen who sleep just beyond his bedroom wall in the dorm his parents oversee, no sisters — there are two now — crying or demanding attention, no raised voice of Stepfather. No sound of Stepfather's steps approaching his room in the night.

Most nights, he waits until either Stepfather has come and gone from his bed or he is absolutely certain that Stepfather is too tired or too drunk to come at all, and he escapes to this place for a couple of hours with his Itty Bitty Book Light and his mother's hand-me-down copy of *The Dark Is Rising*. And although he doesn't really read (he's read it at least a dozen times by now), he enjoys the glow from the small, hot light reflecting off the well-loved pages, shining around his little tent and up into the trees and the vine that is doing its damnedest to kill them.

SCHOOL NIGHT

"JESUS, DOMINIC, have you been smoking? What were you thinking? Goddammit, where were you?"

The boy is back home, seated at the kitchen table, tired, dirty, nauseous, head down. They never found him or his tent, but eventually the boy became too anxious to remain out in the woods. His mother expresses nothing but exhausted relief when she returns home to find the boy sitting in the kitchen. Stepfather is furious.

It's well after baby sister's bedtime, nearly midnight on a school night, and all the boy's fault. The baby is crying upstairs as the boy's mother attempts to soothe her, despite her own tears. The teachers and students who assisted with the search have returned to their dorms and homes, the teachers grateful for their beds, the students grateful for the belated lights out.

Now it's just the boy and Stepfather at the kitchen table, Stepfather at its head, the boy at its side, intently studying the tabletop. There is the glass of Jack Daniels and there is the filterless cigarette poised over the ashtray, and if the boy is exposed to any more smoke this evening, he will surely be sick. But he has not been excused. He will silently endure for as long as necessary.

"Never mind," Stepfather spits in disgust through a cloud of exhaled smoke. "Go to bed. We'll talk about this tomorrow. And you will go to school, and you will return home immediately. Look at me." A pause while he stares at the boy. "We're very disappointed in you." Another pause while he makes sure the boy gets it. "Go."

Careful to maintain the proper persona of shame, the boy gratefully goes. That night, for the first time in weeks, he sleeps soundly.

AMERICAN HISTORY

IN 1990, SEVENTH through twelfth graders in the Litchfield public system begin their school day one full period earlier than the younger students. The difference is only fifty minutes, but it almost ruins the boy's seventh-grade school year. Although the school where he lives is less than ten minutes by car from the school where he studies, he and his fellow faculty brats reside on a long regional bus route that circles for more than an hour before finally depositing them in front of the squat, concrete building that facilitates their education, so unlike the remodeled colonial mansions that house them.

The bus passes by the boy's home at six in the morning. Although two miles separate the school where he lives from the school where he studies, he discovers early in the year that he can get a few extra minutes of sleep if he skips the bus and walks. As long as he leaves the house by 6:30, he'll make first period. But he almost never wakes up before 6:30.

He has American history first period, and he misses so many classes that he's nearly prevented from moving on to eighth grade. The class is taught by Mr. McGurk, a Vietnam veteran rumored to have a metal plate in his head. His face is covered by a wild white beard attempting, unsuccessfully, to conceal a neck wattled with scar tissue. There's about an inch of hairless space by each of his ears, where his sideburns ought to be. Apparently, the metal plate was inserted on one side of his head and no hair will grow there. He shaves the other side to match.

The boy and his fellow students skip the Mister and simply call him McGurk. McGurk is a quietly odd man who presents a stern and unapproachable exterior. Without ever raising his voice, he inspires silent respect bordering on terror in his students. The boy is no exception. In the backward logic of an exhausted, fearful twelve-year-old, the boy skips McGurk's class altogether when he knows he'll be late rather than risk drawing his attention.

During the holidays, McGurk and his wife manically decorate their house and bake thousands upon thousands of Christmas cookies. They open their home to the community, inviting everyone to join them for cookies and cocoa on the weekends between Thanksgiving and Christmas. In McGurk's home, this stern wounded warrior becomes all welcoming smiles behind a Santa beard, thrilled when his modest house fills up with all the kids in town for a few weekends.

The boy's mother calls him McGurkus Circus, a characterization the boy initially finds funny. Later, he will come to consider it rather mean, although he'll allow that she meant it lightly.

His mother gets to know McGurk better than the boy's other teachers, of course, because the boy's plan has failed. Although just a public school in the midst of so many lauded private institutions, the Litchfield system is commonly referred to as The Public Prep School, proudly emphasizing its commitment to individual students' needs as evidenced by its Blue Ribbon status; self-assured in its bloated tax base despite its lack of endowment and dependence on the state. Besides, how could the boy go unnoticed in a seventh-grade class of sixty?

The more he misses McGurk's class, the more McGurk's attention focuses on him. McGurk begins following up with personal phone calls to the boy's mother. As the school year drags on and on and the boy's absences continue to pile up, his academic performance slides past barely acceptable. Conversely, stern, unapproachable McGurk takes more and more interest in the boy.

He can't be sure of what McGurk discusses with his mother or whether she names him Circus for any reason beyond his odd mannerisms, but he does know that McGurk is the only reason he is allowed to complete seventh grade. McGurk grants the boy a B in American history that he's certain he doesn't deserve, and for better or worse the situation never goes beyond McGurk's classroom.

The decision is only made at the end of the year, however, just a couple of weeks ahead of summer break. Before it becomes apparent that the boy will in fact pass, his mother and Stepfather unite in their fury at him. A particularly harsh lecture results from his mother's finally informing Stepfather of the trouble the boy has brought on himself.

A rare dinner at home is finished and cleaned up and both the boy's sisters have been put to bed. The boy is left alone to face his parents in the kitchen. The table is rectangular, pressed lengthwise against the kitchen wall. Stepfather sits at the head, his mother at the foot, and the boy is on the side. They flank him, forcing him to turn from one to the other as they express their disappointment.

He takes it as best he can, helpless to offer any reason for his absenteeism or his poor grades, but at one point he finally unleashes his temper. He points at Stepfather and shouts, "It's all his fault!"

But the boy doesn't have the courage to take the accusation any further than that. His mother apparently chalks it up to normal youthful rebellion. Stepfather reacts with a fury the boy has never imagined.

After throwing his half-hearted accusation, the boy finds Stepfather's change in tone deeply frightening. Stepfather becomes quiet and cold. To fill the void Stepfather's silence creates, the boy's mother uncharacteristically does most of the talking.

"Don't you see that there are consequences to your actions, Dominic? Don't you understand that we can't just let this slide? How do you expect to get into a decent prep school this way?" And the worst, "Don't you know that you can't blame your problems on others?" The questions come one after the other, parroting Stepfather's long-established vocabulary.

Stepfather looks on silently. Stepfather reclines in his chair at the head of the kitchen table, legs crossed, his glass of Jack Daniels and an ashtray placed just so, near his elbow, a filterless Marlboro in his hand. Stepfather smokes that cigarette so deliberately, a drag, a drink, a tap into the ashtray, a drag, a drink, a tap, letting the boy's mother talk. The boy remains imbued with the tiniest spark of defiance, and he meets

Stepfather's eyes as his mother explains why the boy must be punished, deliberately looking away from her as she asks that question, "Don't you know that you can't blame your problems on others?"

But as the boy regards Stepfather's coldness and takes in his silence, he realizes that he is in serious trouble for tossing that accusation. His brief stab at rebellion withers away, replaced by fear. He wants to run.

But where?

STUDY ABROAD

THE FAMILY WOULD normally spend the entire summer visiting Stepfather's parents in Bridgehampton. From there they'd take side trips to Martha's Vineyard or Nantucket or coastal Maine. The boy lives for summer. His step-grandparents welcome the boy as their own grandson. Grandpa happily spends all day sailing with the boy, teaching him how to tie knots or shuck oysters while pointing out coveted larger sloops and catboats. On bad sailing days, they bury themselves in Grandpa's workshop, where he helps the boy paint lead soldiers or build model boats. Occasionally Grandpa forces the boy to help tend to his beloved asparagus patch. During the summer, it is the boy's only chore.

Grandpa is a retired stockbroker, a retired farmer, and a retired colonel who fought in The War. He is an alum of Saint Paul's School, and at dinner the family eats on fine-veined, pale red china depicting scenes from the campus during the 1930s, when Grandpa studied and lived there.

But before dinner, Grandpa drags out a monstrous binder and invites the boy to sit next to him on the couch while he tracks his investments. Grandpa hands the boy a huge calculator that actually prints numbers on a spool of paper and recites figures for the boy to add or subtract while Grandpa sips at his Bloody Mary, smokes his pipe, and makes notations. When the job is done, Grandpa asks the boy to initial the paper trail the calculator spat out. That way, Grandpa says, the government will know who to contact in case they have questions.

Grandpa calls the boy's grandmother Tough Cookie. Grandma is always badgering Grandpa and the boy to come inside, to get off the boat or out of the workshop or garden, to join her, lemonade waiting for the boy and a Bloody Mary for Grandpa. Along with beverages, she has sugar cookies and bologna and cheese sandwiches ready for the boy and his grandfather when they finally come inside. The boy hates bologna, it reminds him of Kathy, but he loves Grandma's sandwiches for their dense slices of white Pepperidge Farm bread and cheap American cheese, sticking in his teeth and molding to the roof of his mouth. Occasionally Grandpa leans close to the boy's ear as they eat and loudly whispers, "She's a Tough Cookie, but they're the only ones worth keeping around." Grandma always hears, and she always smiles.

Stepfather becomes a different person in his parent's home. While the family is there, Stepfather spends his days on landscaping jobs and his nights playing music with old friends. Besides family days at the beach, Stepfather is rarely present. The boy's bedroom adjoins his grandparent's room, and he never worries about late night visits from Stepfather while visiting.

Recently, however, his grandparents have decided to sell the Bridgehampton homestead and move to Litchfield. The Hampton house has become too expensive, and besides, they want to be closer to their grandchildren as they age, closer to the boy.

As a result, his mother and Stepfather have planned a different family vacation to kick off the summer. They intend to drive the family to Portland, Maine, and take the overnight ferry to Nova Scotia. They will drive all the way north to Cape Breton Island. The family will spend two weeks there and then make their way back down the coast to end up in Long Island, where they will stay another week, enjoying the warmer ocean waters while renting a family friend's house not far from the recently vacated homestead.

The trip has been discussed extensively all year. It will be the boy's first time visiting a different country. He's learned that some Cape Breton towns are French-speaking, and French is his favorite subject. He's been studying it every school day for three years. He can't wait to try his skills in the real world. And moose will be everywhere. The boy is desperately excited.

NEOSPORIN

NOW, SITTING AT THE kitchen table between his parents, watching Stepfather slowly smoke his cigarette as his mother continues berating him, the boy learns that he won't be accompanying the family to Nova Scotia. In an eerily deliberate, cold voice, Stepfather finally speaks, informing the boy that he will stay behind with his grandparents in Litchfield. Perhaps that will teach the boy the importance of meeting his obligations.

Normally, the prospect of being away from Stepfather for a solid two weeks would come as an appreciated respite. In this moment, however, nothing seems so cruelly unfair. The wonderful relief of those long Hampton summers, spent in the safety of his grandparent's home, is no more. But Stepfather becomes a different person on vacation, even without Grandma and Grandpa's influence, almost always manically fun. Besides, if the boy shares a hotel room with his sister, it eliminates Stepfather's opportunity to visit the boy's bed.

Later that night, Stepfather will show the boy what to expect if he ever dares to come so close to exposing his secret again.

The boy has a scab on his penis, the result of Stepfather's visit to his room a few nights earlier. Sometimes the boy has trouble ejaculating, and Stepfather will not stop until the boy comes. Sometimes the boy is chafed. Usually when this happens, it means a break of at least a week until the next late-night visit. The boy experiences an odd blend of relief and horror on those mornings when he discovers himself bloody and scabbed. The nights after are some of the best sleep he has over the course of the long school year.

But not this night. The boy has a substantial scab, in the same place

31

as always, the exact spot where Stepfather's index finger wraps around the boy's penis. The boy often thinks that he should just reach down and move that finger slightly when he feels it chafing. But it's a useless thought. To do so would mean breaking his stoic stillness during the act, and that is simply impossible. No amount of pain could make the boy move a muscle during Stepfather's late-night visits, no matter whether caused by a horrible foot or leg cramp, which occurs without fail, or a bleeding penis.

The Nova Scotia discussion ends with the boy's mother tearfully agreeing that the boy will not be allowed to go. She promptly leaves the kitchen, heading to bed. Stepfather sends the boy to his own bed. The boy feels sure that Stepfather won't be visiting his room—he's scabbed, after all. In fact, considering that his mother has only just retired and had been so involved in the lecture, the boy is nearly certain that he is safe for the night.

He's just drifting off to sleep when he hears Stepfather striding down the hall. The boy becomes instantly alert, although as usual he pretends to sleep. When Stepfather enters the bedroom, he calls the boy by name. Normally, Stepfather's tone would be completely different from the anger expressed during his lecture. Normally, his tone would be conciliatory, even kind. This time, that quiet rage the boy had seen at the end of the discussion remains.

"Dominic," Stepfather says, quietly but sternly. "Dominic, I know you're awake. Answer me."

"Dad?" the boy asks, trying to feign sleepiness convincingly.

"Move over," Stepfather says, already climbing into the boy's narrow twin bed. The boy silently complies.

"Get out of these," Stepfather says, once he's next to the boy, tugging at the boy's boxers with his thickly calloused drummer's fingertips. The boy quickly slides his underwear down his legs. This is a new, unexpected dynamic, totally unlike the usual scenario. The boy is scared. He responds promptly.

As soon as the boy has kicked out of his shorts, Stepfather takes the boy's penis firmly in his hand. Stepfather's face is directly next to the boy's, his lips brushing the boy's ear. The boy smells Jack Daniels on Stepfather's breath, overwhelming, intoxicating, sour.

He will never forget the pain as his scab crunched apart under Stepfather's big, calloused hand. He will revisit that sensation viscerally, daily, every time he inspects the scar that he will carry for the rest of his life.

Somehow, despite the terrible burning sensation as the boy's scab tears off, Stepfather makes the boy hard with just a few quick strokes. There, however, the boy's emotional response kicks in. He cannot come. The boy knows that doing so will end it, and he desperately wants to end it, but he simply cannot.

Stepfather works the boy's penis strictly with his hand for what seems all night. Stepfather says things to the boy, "Doesn't that feel good?" and "I'm going to make you come," and "You are going to come," over and over again. The boy never responds in any way. It seems to last forever, and still the boy cannot satisfy him. The boy can no longer feel anything below his waist. He senses moisture but can't be sure whether it's his own blood or Stepfather's come. Stepfather's penis is very close to the boy's, after all, and Stepfather often comes while getting the boy off.

Finally, Stepfather takes the boy in his mouth. Finally, the boy comes.

Stepfather leaves immediately without another word. The boy hears Stepfather running water and spitting in the bathroom across the hall. The boy imagines Stepfather rinsing the boy's blood out of his mouth. Finally, the boy hears the creaking stairs as Stepfather climbs to the bedroom he shares with the boy's mother and baby sister. The boy turns his head and discovers that his pillow is wet, and he realizes that he has been crying. He is unable to move. Eventually he sleeps.

The boy wakes up the next morning in exactly the same position, flat on his back, arms at his sides, fists still clenched. His feet are curled and hopelessly cramped. His sheets are sculpted into stiff peaks by dried, dark red blood. His face is chapped with tears.

As soon as the boy manages to rub the cramps out of his feet, he pulls on pajamas, careful to avoid touching or looking anywhere below his waist. He gathers up the sheets and throws them away, not in the house trash, but outside, in the dumpster behind the parking lot.

The boy is up in plenty of time to make first period. Instead, he takes a shower, remakes his bed with fresh sheets, and climbs back in for an hour. He doesn't sleep. The shower hurt terribly, and the boy cannot bring himself to look.

Later, as he dresses for school, he finally forces himself to see. The boy inspects his penis, swollen to such a degree that he has difficulty pulling up his jeans. It's bruised black and oozing blood and puss from the wound, which has grown substantially.

He sheds involuntary tears when he manages to zip his pants shut. Indescribably terrified, he is certain that he is permanently damaged and that he needs a doctor. The boy briefly considers going to his mother. He immediately discards the thought. How to begin to explain? And even if he somehow managed, who could say what the consequences would be?

Over the following weeks, he will treat the wound the only way he knows, with peroxide soaked cotton balls and Neosporin, and eventually it will heal. Not well—he will always have the scar, and the skin just below the head of his penis will always be weirdly loose, noticeably disfigured when it isn't erect. Even when hard, there will still be a discernible line marking where the damage was done, a reminder that will haunt every intimate moment in the years to come.

SEX ED

MCGURK ULTIMATELY passes the boy. Stepfather relents when the decision is made, and the boy is allowed to accompany the family on vacation.

During that vacation, the boy encounters the most beautiful girl he's ever seen, working at a general store on Cape Breton Island, just down the street from the cottage the family has rented. He visits the store every day, ignoring Stepfather's thrifty criticism, spending his allowance on penny candy, the incredible anticipation of his hands meeting the girl's as he passes over his coins exceeded only by their perfunctory exchange of greetings:

"Merci!"

"Merci beaucoup!"

In the years to come, the boy will forget her name—something exotically French in stark juxtaposition to the awful American country music perpetually playing in the store—but he will never forget her smile, her bemused eyes, so clearly aware of the boy's desperate young crush, her pixyish haircut and short T-shirts advertising her pierced belly button and bands he'd never heard of, *so cool*. Without her, the boy wouldn't have learned that he could masturbate to completion without Stepfather's aid. At least, not for awhile.

The boy feels certain that Stepfather will never touch him again.

The boy will cherish the memories of those brief conversations in French, his quick glimpses of moose along the Cabot Trail, and those weeks of uninterrupted sleep, lulled by the brisk, salty north Atlantic air and his little sister's snores each night in the safe, cozy room they shared. And while at the time he hated to imagine being discovered in

35

the act, he'll find comfort in the memories of the many-more-showers-than-necessary he took during those weeks, discovering pleasure in his own body for the first time, safe in the privacy of his bedroom's en-suite bathroom, safe in the privacy of fantasies all his own, the sound of his movements hidden beneath the roar of water coursing through the cottage's exposed pipes, the evidence of his pleasure immediately washed away.

Other than his newly discovered ability to masturbate, the boy won't remember any particular change in his behavior, but perhaps that was enough. Perhaps the discovery of this private act represented as much a marker of growth as his advanced height or his ever-more-defined musculature or his ever-spreading body hair.

Perhaps it changed his pheromones. Perhaps Stepfather could smell the change. Perhaps it repulsed him.

For whatever reason, just as he'd predicted, Stepfather would never attempt to touch the boy again. There was no confrontation, no acknowledgment, nothing discussed, nothing to mark an end.

Fitting, of course, because that wasn't the end at all.

STUDIO ART

THE BOY ACHIEVES his adult height of six feet, three inches shortly after turning thirteen. Until the age of sixteen, his deepest desire is to shrink.

His mother has also grown. Now chair of the art department, she curates the school's gallery, showcasing artists associated with the school and the local community, sometimes even contemporary professionals from New York or Boston or beyond. She insists that her son accompany her to art show openings, which never fail to attract large crowds. His mother is well aware of the boy's shyness. He continually surprises her by never hesitating to agree.

Stepfather has no patience for art shows, even though he is a musician, an artist himself, and his wife, a painter, has devoted much of her life to the development and display of creative work. Stepfather's contempt becomes particularly venomous at the prospect of attending openings, with their bacon-wrapped scallops and miniature toothpicked hot dogs, their white wine in plastic cups and small square napkins. These snobberies are beneath Stepfather. He makes no effort to avoid disparaging people who enjoy such nonsense, ignoring his wife's face as it falls.

The boy recalls the last time Stepfather attended an opening. He'd come to the decision suddenly, one of his manic whims that left no time to arrange a babysitter. The whole family attends, including the boy's sisters, now ages four and eight. They all arrive together, just early enough to set up the food and wine before showgoers arrive. As usual, the chore is left to the boy.

As he finishes arranging the table, obsessively centering a platter of crudités just *so*, he notices that most of the miniature hot dogs have already disappeared, marring his carefully executed spread before the night has even begun. Looking for a replacement, he finds Stepfather in the gallery's kitchen, leaning his obesity against a stainless steel table, a cocktail napkin overflowing with tiny hot dogs clutched in that big, calloused drummer's hand. He shoves them into his mouth one after the other, flicking his spent toothpicks to the floor for the boy to sweep up later.

"God, how I hate these events," Stepfather declares through his chomping mouth, gesturing with a hot dog toward the swinging door and the gallery beyond. He briefly regards the wiener before sucking it off its toothpick. "But these are great!"

Minutes after the show opens to the public, the boy's precocious little sister, the eight-year-old, loudly declares to one of her parents' female colleagues, "My Daddy says you're, like, orca-fat!"

The boy will never forget Stepfather's tone, his sheer meanness when, just an hour before that opening, he declared his fellow teacher, one of his wife's few friends, "orca-fat." He'd been dressing and loudly complaining that none of his clothes fit.

As always, Stepfather's presence suffuses the entire house, infecting the whole family even from the confines of his closet. The boy and his sisters wait in the kitchen while their mother stands by the door, all four of them fully dressed, ready to go. The boy will remember his mother's leg twitching and twisting with impatience, her car keys jangling in one hand, the other clutching the door knob.

"You always look great, honey!" she calls, her tone revealing no hint of her displeasure. "Almost ready?"

"At least I don't look like Barb! She's, like, *orca-fat!*" Stepfather shouts back, his harsh chuckle unforgettably ugly.

Now Stepfather uses his daughters as an excuse to remain at home, decrying the expense of babysitters, magnanimously offering the boy and his mother a date night at each new opening. He insists that the girls *just aren't up for it.*

"Go on without us, Sissy, we'll be fine," Stepfather assures her. "Take the boy! You two could use some fun together. What is there to eat

38

around here?" he asks. "Bring home some of those little wieners, will you?"

The boy seizes these opportunities, happy to participate in Stepfather's not-so-subtle manipulation, grateful for the excuse of an evening spent beyond his grasp.

And the boy genuinely enjoys the openings. He loves bacon-wrapped scallops. He appreciates the opportunity to surreptitiously sip a little wine, enjoying the way the plastic cup breaks into thin, sharp shards as he kneads its edges.

Mostly, he appreciates the quiet ritual, the slow pace of walking, and that it's perfectly acceptable to sit quietly and stare for a long while. He quickly learns how to appear totally immersed in art, whether he likes it or not. When conversation interrupts, it's generally muted and quickly concluded.

Of course, a certain amount of dialogue is unavoidable. His mother enjoys showing her son off to her colleagues and artist friends, who inevitably exclaim over his height and how much older he seems, how well mannered, well spoken, and handsome he is.

"This is my beautiful baby boy!" she announces, too loudly, reaching up to rub his shoulder in quick nervous circles. The boy smiles politely, mutters his thank-yous, and wishes for them all to look away. As quickly as possible, he finds a piece of art to stare at. He sits quietly, immersed, aloof.

He wants to be invisible.

FLIGHT OF THE ALBATROSS

IN THE YEARS TO COME, the boy will remember Barbara. He will painfully recall her effort to laugh at Stepfather's words, thoughtlessly parroted through his daughter's mouth. The boy will hope that his remembrance honors her helpless struggle that night, as she tried to rise above being the butt of that cruel joke.

He will remember seeing her lose that battle, failing to suppress her shocked tears, how she abruptly turned and fled the gallery, nearly jogging by the time she reached the exit. He will remember his sister's confusion, how she in turn burst into tears, yet another casualty of Stepfather's callousness.

A few months after that opening, Barbara will leave her teaching position at the school altogether, well before the end of the academic year. The boy's mother will give him a copy of Barbara's recently published novel. He'll quickly forget the story, but its title will linger, a haunting reminder of his deepest desire at that age: Flight of the Albatross.

The boy will often wonder what hidden details, what outside insight into his family a conversation with Barbara—another of Stepfather's victims, a woman who felt compelled to title her novel after one of the world's widest-ranging birds, one of literature's classically recognized metaphors, the heavy, far-flown albatross—might reveal.

RESEARCH METHODS

WITH SURPRISINGLY little difficulty the boy locates his father, his *real* Dad. The boy has no recollection of Cumberland, Maryland, the small city where he was born, but his mother remembers it well. She quickly confirms that the boy's father still lives there. When the boy calls information and speaks his father's full name aloud for the first time, *William Anthony Miller*, the operator promptly offers a phone number. The boy asks the operator to repeat the number, unsure that he has heard correctly. The last four digits are his mother's and Stepfather's home number, perfectly reversed.

The boy is filled with uncertainty. He has no idea how he feels about contacting his father, his conflicting emotions all tangled up beneath a blanket of anxiety so heavy he can't begin to identify what lies beneath.

He is fifteen years old. It's been eleven years since he last encountered his father, a meeting hazy in his memory. He consistently dreams of lots of curly dark hair and huge dark glasses but remembers little else.

The boy did not instigate the search for his father. More and more often, Stepfather has been losing patience with the boy's perpetual silence in his presence, the constant attempts at avoidance, the boy's "disappearing act," as Stepfather calls it.

Recently, Stepfather declared, "If you're going to act like a guest in my house, you might as well become one in truth." And, turning to the boy's mother, "Sissy, I think it's time we got the boy in touch with his father. Maybe we can at least get some damn child support out of this situation."

The boy does not want to be a guest in his house. The boy wishes with all his heart that he could be like his precocious little sister, now nine years old and immeasurably stronger than the boy. She sings with her father, she laughs with him, even at him, she makes fun and makes demands and never fails to get what she wants. She appears totally unconcerned when Stepfather is angry with her. She simply yells right back.

The boy is unable to do any of these things. He's barely able to speak with Stepfather, let alone sing or laugh or yell. How deeply he envies his sister. He can only shrink.

The boy has been walking around with his father's phone number in his pocket for nearly a week now. The number is written on a thick scrap torn from one of his mother's expensive little notebooks of handmade paper. The boy folds the paper and keeps it in his leather billfold, a treasured hand-me-down from his grandfather, enjoying the way it makes the wallet feel thick, substantial, like it's full of cash.

At least once each day, he takes the paper out, unfolds it, and studies the numbers. He repeats those last four digits in his head, back and forth, seven-two-four-four, four-four-two-seven, seven-two-four-four, four-four-two-seven, again and again. He has yet to make the call.

At the end of the week, Stepfather approaches the boy as he sweeps the kitchen floor, finishing the nightly chores.

"Did you call him?" he asks, clearly expecting the obvious answer.

"Not yet," the boy whispers.

"What? Speak up, dammit!"

"Not yet!" the boy tries again.

"Why not?"

"I don't know."

"Jesus fucking Christ, Dominic. Okay. Let's go." Stepfather yanks the broom from the boy's hands, propelling him toward the phone.

"Call him," Stepfather demands.

"Right now?" the boy asks, fear suddenly inflecting his voice. He breaks out in sweat. He looks at the clock hanging above the phone. It's just about quarter past seven.

"Yes, goddammit! Right now!"

Ever so slowly, the boy picks up the phone and dials his father's number from memory, barely catching himself before inverting those last four digits, seven-two-four-four. The boy can feel Stepfather's breath on his neck, measured, heavy, and hot.

The phone rings twice. The receiver on the other end is picked up. There is a long pause. The boy's anxiety peaks. Finally—

"Hello?" A reedy male voice, obviously old.

"Hello, um, is Mr. Miller there?" the boy croaks.

"Say again?" loudly, nearly a yell. The boy flinches.

"Speak up!" Stepfather hisses at his neck.

"Is Mr. Miller there?" the boy repeats, forcing his voice louder, slower.

"Which one?"

"Uh, Bill? Bill Miller?"

"Who's calling?"

"This is Dominic," the boy's full name suddenly a source of confusion, "Dominic, uh, Marshall."

"Dominic?" the reedy voice is suddenly shocked. "You're Dominic?"

"Yes. This is Dominic," the boy repeats. That much of his name, at least, is clear.

"Dominic. Oh my god," the man chuckles a little. "I'm your grandfather."

CROSS COUNTRY

THE BOY SPEAKS with his father later that night, after his newly discovered grandfather delivers his message. The conversation is unbearably awkward, surreal, the words exchanged immediately slipping from the boy's memory.

But he will remember forging ahead despite his anxiety. He will remember acting out of character, with an unaccustomed pushiness, perhaps modeled on his little sister, suddenly shining through. He demands a meeting as soon as possible. His father promptly agrees.

His father sounds genuinely excited, even giddy. The immediately positive response overwhelms the boy. He's never experienced anything like this, never even imagined what such a thing might feel like. His father wants to see him, and soon. His *real* Dad.

His father continues, promising to make travel arrangements and wire money so the boy can visit Maryland, profusely apologetic that he can't immediately come to Connecticut. The boy barely registers his father's words.

"Thank you so much," he says, before hanging up the phone.

The following day, the boy goes for a long run. He achieves the clarity that only comes after a few miles have passed beneath his feet. He pulls back a corner of that blanket of anxiety that's been hanging over him throughout that long week, finally discovering what lay beneath: desperation.

But underneath that desperation, even further down, in his deepest, darkest, most effectively smothered corner, there is, perhaps, something small, something that fears revealing too much of itself. It's just a glimmer, a tiny spark, such an unfamiliar sensation, but it is decidedly there: hope.

As he runs, the boy smiles. Despite the distance he's already covered, his feet begin turning over more quickly, effortlessly bouncing off the pavement, propelling him forward.

SOMETHING WICKED
THIS WAY COMES

THOSE EARLY TEENAGE years are dominated by the imperative to avoid Stepfather, a goal that relentlessly motivates the boy. He packs his schedule to exhaustion with school, sports, and extracurricular activities, constantly seeking a deadened state of sleep at the end of each long day, desperately attempting to mitigate the insomnia that has pursued him from childhood. He creates excuses to retire to bed before Stepfather returns home in the evening, to rise well before Stepfather in the morning. Soon he will discover drugs and alcohol. But for now, the boy pursues oblivion through more wholesome means.

Joining the cross-country team back in fifth grade introduced the boy to the incomparable therapy of running, well before he was fully grown. Now he runs daily, in addition to school-sanctioned practices, in all seasons, whatever the weather. Hour after hour, he throws one foot in front of the other, eating as much distance as fast as he can, a hundred miles a week and more.

Besides offering an excuse to leave the house almost anytime, the boy's running practice serves other purposes. It provides temporary relief from his constant anxiety, replacing it with an addictive though fleeting sense of euphoria. It strengthens his body while keeping him as small as he can possibly be, and it rewards him with a rare sense of satisfied achievement. Most important, nothing ensures sleep like a fifteen-mile run.

When not lost in his runner's high, the boy is a powerless, anxious wreck. Eventually he must return home, and he must do so ahead of Stepfather. Entering the house to find Stepfather already there eliminates the opportunity to anticipate his mood and react accordingly. Luckily, Stepfather often departs for the evening after a brief meal, gigging with fellow musicians when his presence isn't required at the school. The boy spends his days predicting Stepfather's schedule, altering his own in opposition. Mostly, he is successful. Sometimes, he is not.

The boy possesses a supernatural awareness of Stepfather's approach. The family dog, a blocky black Lab named Skye, cocks her head and dances in a circle long moments after the boy has already detected Stepfather's returning car. The specific squeak of brakes at the stop sign a block away. The shift from first to second gear as Stepfather completes the turn at the top of the street. The tires hitting the gravelly spot at the bottom of the driveway in the exact same way every time. Stepfather's particular manner of slamming his car door quickly, followed by his heavy steps in the breezeway. His exaggerated sighing as he enters the kitchen. His immediate demand for his wife's attention.

"Sissy!" he calls without fail, inserting a long *a* before the *y*, *Sissay*, the end drawn out, punctuated by the kitchen door slamming shut behind him. The boy gauges the poles of Stepfather's mood with near-perfect accuracy based on the pitch of that single utterance. Is it happily loud, exuberant? Perhaps avoidance is unnecessary. Is it tired, is there any hint of annoyance? Disappear.

Of course, by the time Stepfather calls his wife, it's too late to escape. But the boy can even gauge something of Stepfather's coming mood based on variations in the sound of his approaching car. Does he shift abruptly, is he driving too fast? Not good. If possible, depart immediately.

From that first moment of awareness, the boy has nearly a full minute to leave the house. Usually there's just enough time to throw on his running shoes or at least grab Skye's leash for a walk, a chore the boy can't be criticized for seeing to.

Sometimes, however, Stepfather drives too fast. The boy can't make his escape in time, he will be caught in the breezeway or the driveway or even flagged down in the street. In his constant search for books that offer alternate realities, the boy has recently discovered Bradbury's *Something Wicked This Way Comes*. In these moments, the phrase eclipses all other thoughts in his mind.

So the boy hides in the bathroom, futilely hoping that Stepfather won't seek him out. The boy drops his pants and sits on the toilet, his commitment to this charade total. He leans forward, places his elbows on his knees, clasps his hands between his legs, and lifts his heels off the floor just enough to make the nerves in his calves jump. His face strains with feigned effort. No audience will ever appreciate his perfect performance.

A basket of magazines sits underneath the sink directly opposite the toilet. Not wanting to make any sound that might be interpreted as leisurely, the boy never flips through them, but he memorizes their covers. The J. Crew and L. L. Bean catalogues sport well-dressed, fit, chisel-faced men, totally unlike obese, frumpy Stepfather. *Connecticut Magazine* and *Architectural Digest* display privileged, unsmiling families from Greenwich and Manhattan and even his hometown, all dressed in tennis white. His mother's favorite, the British edition of *House Beautiful*, is printed on wonderfully thick matte paper that smells something like cedar.

The boy may hide in the bathroom for half an hour or more, staring at those magazines through squinted eyes. Should Stepfather call for him, he will reply in an artfully strained voice that he doesn't feel well. The boy is rarely ill, and Stepfather knows it, but the boy's complete immersion in his performance is so convincing that, suddenly, it becomes truth. Sometimes the boy manages to squeeze out an audible fart. Sometimes Stepfather leaves the boy to his act.

The boy notes every new speck of dirt and cobweb on the black tiled floor and leaves them all right where they are, marking their incremental growth between the monthly cleanings that are the boy's responsibility. He observes wavy splotches on the magazine covers, accumulated spray from the toilet's flush marring those perfect, wealthy Connecticut faces. Stepfather never closes the lid.

Eventually, Stepfather will note the filth. Any day now, he will remind the boy to add the bathroom to his regular chore routine. He will remind the boy that he shouldn't have to remind the boy. The boy will wait for the reminder, a pitifully tiny rebellion that only invites more anxiety.

The boy's legs fall asleep. The toilet presses a red ring into his skin. When Stepfather departs or the boy simply can't stand to sit on the toilet for another moment, he finally stands, twists, checks out his red-ringed ass in the mirror, and thinks, *This is your life*.

Occasionally, Stepfather, having brought home a particularly black mood, loses patience with the charade. He pounds on the bathroom door, demanding that the boy emerge, drawing confrontation in a dark inversion of a mother drawing her child's bath. Helpless, the boy must comply, but still he delays, finishing his Oscar-worthy act, slowly wiping his ass, closing the lid, flushing the toilet, then thoroughly washing, rinsing, and drying his hands on a towel monogrammed with Stepfather's initials. The boy refolds the towel in thirds before replacing it on its rack, careful to center those initials so that they are perfectly displayed.

Finally, slowly, the boy unlocks the door, opening it ever so slightly. Stepfather immediately throws the door wide, grabbing the boy by the wrist, propelling him through the living room, steering him through the dining room, a shove to the shoulder, into the kitchen, finally to the wall phone, forcing the boy to call his *real* Dad to demand delivery of the now expected but perpetually late child support check.

Stepfather stands just behind the boy with his hands on his hips, shaking his head, muttering in elaborate disgust as the boy hesitantly dials his father's number. The boy's mother quietly prepares dinner, head down, myopically focused on the stovetop, stirring something, anything, the back of her head inscrutable.

The boy finally finishes dialing and silently prays for the answering machine.

He will remember many such evenings, countless forced phone calls. He will remember his gratitude for his father's busy restaurant schedule, keeping him at work through most evenings, safely away from his home phone. The boy will remember his fear at being caught in the pretense that he was forbidden from calling his father at his restaurant, where the boy would be sure to reach him. The boy will wonder why he felt the need to protect his father, why he avoided that conversation when it may have ended his own ordeal.

The boy will remember Stepfather's making him repeatedly call his father's home anyway, knowing that the boy's father would be away late into the night, tirelessly forcing the boy back to the phone again and again, every half hour, interrupting dinner, dragging the boy from his bedroom, physically placing the receiver in his hand, often dialing the number for the boy, until finally, finally Stepfather grew weary, finally he felt that the boy had left enough mortified messages for one night. The boy will never forget Stepfather shaking his head, angry and disgusted, muttering about deadbeat dads as he dismissed the boy to his room.

DO ANDROIDS DREAM OF
ELECTRIC SHEEP?

WELL OF COURSE THEY DO, the boy thinks, studying the book's cover, *just like I dream about my father's crazy hair*. He opens the novel to his make-shift bookmark, a thick Polaroid, the only picture his mother could find of his *real* Dad, the long lost father he is finally about to meet. The photo was taken fifteen years ago, in 1978, the year the boy was born. The man in the Polaroid smiles through a thick black beard, his big, heavily tinted glasses framed by a mass of wild, curly hair falling beyond his shoulders. He wears a ruffled red paisley shirt, unbuttoned nearly to his navel, wiry chest hair reaching out from between its wide-open collar.

Luke, I am your father, the boy thinks, imagining a Darth Vader cape onto the man in the photo. But no, this father won't be evil. The boy left all the evil in his life back in Connecticut, early this morning when he boarded the train in New Haven. The boy decides that with all that hair, his father will be a benevolent wizard who will instantly set the boy's whole world aright. The boy removes the Vader cape from his imagination, replacing it with Gandalf's staff. It doesn't seem to fit either.

The boy tucks the Polaroid into the back of his book and tries to focus on reading. He's always wanted to see *Blade Runner*, but his self-enforced rule won't allow him to watch a movie before reading the novel it's based on, if one exists. He was surprised to find that the futuristic film was adapted from a book written in the sixties, and even more surprised to discover its original title: *Do Androids Dream of Electric Sheep?* It is the boy's first introduction to Philip K. Dick, and it is undoubtedly the best title he's ever encountered. All morning, he's been wondering why they chose something as banal as *Blade Runner* to replace it for the movie. Is this something he can discuss with his father?

Is he a reader? the boy wonders for the thousandth time. *Will he think I'm silly for all my fantasy and sci-fi novels, like Stepfather does?*

This sort of question has been rattling around the boy's thoughts for weeks, ever since that first awkward phone call, becoming constant as the hour of meeting finally approaches. *What will we talk about? Will we like the same music? Or will he ridicule mine, like Stepfather? Is he a runner? Does he like tennis? Or is he a baseball-basketball-football kind of guy? Or NASCAR? Please don't let him be a NASCAR kind of guy.*

The boy has been on the train for five hours. Soon he'll arrive in Washington, DC, where he will meet his father and begin collecting answers to all those questions. He stares at the page of his open book. The words run together, as they have all morning. He hasn't managed to get through the first chapter.

For the fifth time since boarding the train he feels the need to pee, a now familiar nervous itch in his bladder that may or may not result in any urine. The boy marks his place, page four, with the Polaroid and stands, begging forgiveness of his neighbor in the aisle seat once again as he shuffles past, lurching toward the restroom.

As anxious as he is about meeting his father, the boy has been thoroughly enjoying himself. It is his first time traveling alone, and he's never experienced freedom like this. Every moment, every simple interaction, from collecting his ticket to buying a cup of coffee to claiming his seat on the train, has been experienced through this new lens of freedom, infused with pure excitement. Stepfather is behind him, in another state, a different world. Suddenly nothing limits or even influences the boy's actions. For the first time, he feels his own autonomy. He can do anything that occurs to him.

New to this feeling, the boy sticks to small stuff, barely exploring his limits. *I want coffee, so I buy coffee,* he says to himself. *I think I may have to pee, so I go to the restroom. I don't ask, I don't worry about what anyone thinks. Because these are things that people do. Amazing.*

Underneath these thoughts is another, too big to fully acknowledge but clamoring to be heard. It is the thought that, if he is brave, he could walk out of the station without meeting his father. He could cash in his return ticket and add the proceeds to the hundred dollars in his wallet, money his father wired, more travel money than he could ever spend in a single trip, a small fortune, really, and disappear somewhere in Washington, DC.

But the thought is too big, too scary. The boy isn't that brave. And besides, he wants to meet his father. He wants answers to all those questions.

So he enjoys his newly discovered freedom in small, safe doses. And he is genuinely thrilled by the idea that tonight he will sleep four hundred miles from Stepfather. There will be no chores, no opportunity for a lecture, nothing to avoid, nothing to lie about. And when he wakes up tomorrow morning, he will still be four hundred miles from Stepfather.

His only remaining obligation is to call his mother when he arrives, just to let her know that he made it to Maryland safely. Even that small chore chafes at the boy's newfound sense of autonomy, but once he has seen to it, he reassures himself, he will be truly free. For three days, anyway. For now, it is enough.

The boy feels the train slow as he finishes washing his hands in the restroom. An intercom dings above his head, and a deep, soothing voice informs him that the Northeastern Express is ten minutes from its final destination, Union Station, DC. Passengers will disembark on the left.

The boy hurries back to his seat to find his neighbor already departed. *Probably didn't want to deal with you forcing his knees to the side again*, he thinks, always conscious of the inconvenience he causes. The boy pulls his overnight bag from the overhead compartment, stuffs his unread book and his unlistened-to Walkman inside, and sits, holding the bag in his lap, looking out the window just as the train enters a black tunnel. He lifts his heels from the floor slightly and feels his legs jump, the anxious habit born of all those hours spent on the toilet while avoiding Stepfather. Should the repetition of that behavior in this new situation, anticipating the fast approaching meeting with his *real* Dad, concern him? He taps his fingers against his bag in time with his jumping legs, an addition to the routine that reminds him, disturbingly, of Stepfather's strong drummer's hands. He studies his reflection in the dark glass. He tries on a smile. It looks hesitant, nervous.

Will he like me? The only question that really matters, forcing all the others aside.

Dim lights appear in the tunnel, and the train slows to a crawl. The tunnel widens into a cavernous space, other train tracks stretching out into the darkness. The boy returns his heels to the floor, forcing his legs to stillness, then his fingers, a futile effort to expel Stepfather from his thoughts.

Finally, the tunnel brightens, and the train lurches to a stop. The intercom dings again, that soothing voice informing passengers of their arrival. "It's *gorgeous* in the capital today, folks, eighty-two degrees and sunny. For those traveling on, arrival and departure information can be found upstairs in the center of *historic* Union Station. Thank you for riding the Northeastern Express and *have yourself a capital day!*"

Thank you, sir, I'll try, the boy silently answers.

He stands as the aisle fills up with passengers preparing to disembark. There is no room for him join them, so the boy balances against his seat, unwilling to sit back down. He suddenly realizes that he's begun to sweat. He can hear his own heavy breathing. He smells something slightly foul and realizes it's his own body odor. *Did I forget deodorant this morning?* he wonders. He takes a deep breath, trying to calm himself, failing.

A smiling woman allows the boy to step into the aisle ahead of her. He nods his thanks, unwilling to risk speaking. His legs feel wooden, locked, unable to properly bend. He waddles up the aisle, trying to keep from bumping into the person in front of him, feeling the nice lady's bag pressing against his back and suddenly hating her. A trickle of sweat streaks down from his armpit, pooling against the waistband of his boxers inside his jeans.

Finally, he is off the train and onto the platform, feeling slightly better now that the press of moving bodies has some space to spread out. He pauses and purposefully shakes his legs, one at a time, trying to loosen them back to their usual elasticity, trying to control his breathing. *My legs feel tight, so I shake them. I'm free*, he reminds himself.

On the phone last night, his father said that he would meet the boy by the main information desk, just inside the entrance. The boy follows his fellow passengers up a long escalator that lands in a wide hallway lined with food kiosks, Sbarro on his right, Au Bon Pain on his left. The boy turns in a full circle, scanning the crowd, trying to decide which way to go.

A sign stating "information" directs him around a corner, and there, across the crowd, is a man wearing a black button-down tucked into jeans, scanning travelers as they come and go. The man's silky-looking shirt is open nearly to his navel. His hair is short and mostly grey, but still curly. His only facial hair is a handlebar mustache and his glasses are smaller, but they are still heavily tinted.

The boy is barely aware of his body's movement as he approaches this strangely familiar stranger. *Just keep walking, just go!* the most subversive part of himself hisses from the back of his mind. The boy smothers the thought.

The man finally notices the boy as he draws near. Their eyes meet.

"Are you Bill Miller?" the boy asks, relieved to find his voice working.

"I am. Are you Dominic?" the man asks.

"I am," the boy says, and sticks out his hand.

The man shakes it firmly, once, twice, then holds the boy's hand still for a long moment. The boy worries that his palm is offensively sweaty. The man abruptly smiles.

"Let's get out of here," he says, releasing the boy's hand and reaching for his bag. "Let me take that."

The boy hands over his bag and follows his father out of the main terminal, through the throngs crowding the entrance, through a set of revolving doors, and out into the sun. His father walks quickly, crossing the wide sidewalk, approaching a two-seater sports car parked illegally among a row of taxis. The boy struggles to follow, his legs stubbornly unwilling to obey. *Last chance*, that subversive voice whispers.

The boy's father looks over his shoulder, still smiling.

"Do you like fast cars?" he asks.

Do androids dream of electric sheep? the phrase floods the boy's mind, instantly shattering his tension and nearly making him laugh aloud.

His father smiles wider in response to the boy's grin.

"Good," he laughs. "We'll be home before you know it. Your grandmother can't wait to see you."

DRIVER'S ED

THE BRIDGEHAMPTON homestead has long since been remodeled
by its new, wealthier owners, but Stepfather isn't interested in vaca-
tioning elsewhere. The rest of the family remembers trips to Nova Scotia and Down East Maine fondly, far more affordable vacations that the
boy's mother hesitantly advocates for, but Stepfather insists on spending a week of each summer revisiting his privileged childhood play-
ground, no matter how much has changed since his youth.

Renting one of his family friend's homes has become financially
impossible. Instead, the family spends the week crowded into a tiny
cottage, one of perhaps half a dozen identical white vinyl structures
clustered around a pool behind a row of motel rooms. A chain-link
fence surrounds the property, the only barrier separating it from the
Montauk Highway, constantly rumbling with traffic passing through
Bridgehampton toward even more expensive addresses in East Hampton and Sag Harbor.

The cottage contains two bedrooms, a bathroom, and an open area
for cooking and sitting. The boy's parents sleep in one bedroom, his
sisters in the other, and the boy spends his nights on the springy pullout couch in the sitting area, coaxing himself awake each day with the
dawn so he can reassure himself that he has not wet the bed. Although
he hasn't embarrassed himself that way in some time, he always worries. More important, he must eliminate any evidence of his rest before
it can be discovered by Stepfather, who might use the excuse of clutter
to lecture the boy.

Every morning, the boy greets his early-rising mother already fully
dressed, his bed neatly folded away, sitting on the reconstructed couch,

a book opened in his hands. The boy's mother offers him coffee while she prepares her own. The boy gladly accepts, enjoying this new token of adultness and the quiet hour spent with his mother, who asks without judgment about whatever fantasy novel he's currently reading.

Now that Hampton summers, once stretching from Memorial Day to Labor Day, have been compressed into a single week, every day is a beach day, an obligation Stepfather insists on fulfilling.

"We're gonna really pack it in!" Stepfather declares, as the family minivan leaves Connecticut behind, crossing into New York, speeding east along the Long Island Expressway. Stepfather's anticipation infects the children, even the boy, but evades his wife, who clutches at her seatbelt and smothers little shrieks as Stepfather swerves through traffic, aggressively eager. Stepfather ignores his wife's discomfort, happily prattling on about sandbars and dunes and horseshoe crabs and arrowheads.

"Maybe we'll even make it over to Lilywhite's, get a few lead soldiers to add to your collection," he calls to the boy in the rear-view mirror, actually smiling as he meets the boy's eyes. "Grandpa would've liked that, right?" The boy nods hopefully, praying that this mood will last.

Once arrived, the family takes Stepfather at his word, preparing for the beach early every day. Stepfather said that mornings would be for the ocean side, where he can really swim while the surf is high. Afternoons will be for the bay side, where the boy's mother, who fears high surf as much as heavy traffic, will be more comfortable wading and beachcombing. The boy loves both, but he's especially excited by the prospect of finding an arrowhead or wampum or a perfect conch shell, far more likely on the bay side.

The boy's mother begins by eight o'clock, preparing breakfast alongside a picnic lunch for later. The sandwiches will become unpleasantly soggy by the time they are finally eaten. Stepfather will eat nothing but canned tuna at the beach, the cheapest possible seafood, smothered in mayonnaise.

The minivan is packed with food and beach supplies by nine, an hour before Stepfather stirs. Once prepared, the boy's mother takes the children to the pool to wait. The boy helps his sisters swim in the shallow end, kneeling in the water while he spins them in increasingly quick circles, each of his forearms clutched by a screeching girl, never failing to scrape the top of his feet or his knees against the rough concrete bottom. Besides the feeling of constant rush and the anxiety of wondering whether he's "packed it in" enough, the boy's lasting memory of the week will be dominated by chlorine, its smell infusing his nose and lingering in his hair, its sting in his cuts and boiling acne, the way it makes his skin feel papery for days after vacation ends.

Stepfather finally emerges from bed. He steps outside wearing nothing but a pair of shorts, his heavy, hairy belly protruding into the light ahead of his features, dark under the shadow cast by the cottage's covered stoop, reflecting his already black mood.

"Sissay!" he yells toward the pool, shading his eyes with one hand, gesturing with the other. "Come on, dammit, we've gotta get moving!" The boy's mother instantly springs to her feet, as attuned to Stepfather's mood as is the boy himself.

"Dominic, baby, get your sisters out of the pool and ready to go," his mother instructs, scrambling to gather her book, her coffee mug. "Your father will want to get to the beach soon." As he has since Stepfather first became Stepfather, the boy lets the misnomer pass, despite having just come from a visit to his *real* Dad.

His mother hurries to the cottage, where Stepfather has already retreated inside, waiting for her to pour him a cup of coffee and make him breakfast. He will play his bodhran, the only drum that would fit for the trip, while waiting to be fed. The boy will remember the staccato sounds drifting from the cottage, complicated rhythms interspersed with a mournful sighing sound, a familiar soundtrack that temporarily eases the boy's anxiety. While Stepfather is so occupied, the boy is safe.

He imagines Stepfather's strong, calloused fingers flying across the drum's head, the brief pause before the sigh, Stepfather quickly licking his thumb before forcing the wet fingertip across the stretched calfskin in a curving arc. Stepfather will likely want a shower and a shave after his practice. The boy continues spinning his sisters—his *half* sisters—in the pool until the music stops.

When Stepfather is finally ready, the family piles into the minivan, parents in the front, sisters in the back, the boy on the third-row seat, in the *way* back, as far from Stepfather as possible, stretching his long legs to the side, his arm resting on the heavy cooler that, soon, he will lug over the dunes to the ocean's edge, a five-minute walk that never fails to feel like an hour.

It's nearly noon, and the boy wonders why they don't just eat now, in the cottage or by the pool or even in the minivan, instead of hauling all that food down to the beach, where they'll end up eating immediately anyway and then waiting the requisite twenty minutes to swim. The tuna's just getting soggier. The boy keeps the thought to himself.

The boy will remember the inevitable lunch discussion, Stepfather's announcement that it was too late to make any other destinations that day. "Let's do better tomorrow, okay, girls? You too, Dominic. You know how your mother loves the bay. And I'd like to make it out to Montauk and maybe Shelter Island at least once."

The boy will remember his eagerness to request a trip to Lilywhite's, the cozily cramped toy store in East Hampton he used to peruse with Grandpa, who joked about diversity in the Hamptons while assuring the boy that it was the only store in America besides F. A. O. Schwartz where real lead soldiers could still be bought.

The boy will make a continuous study of Stepfather's moods, alert for an opportunity to casually mention East Hampton, perhaps the coffee and ice cream shop around the corner from Lilywhite's, the one his mother loves so much, careful to avoid any direct expression of his own desire.

It takes minutes just to turn out of the motel parking lot and join the Montauk Highway's ceaseless stream of traffic. Stepfather becomes increasingly belligerent as he inches the minivan forward in sharp jerks, yelling at cars and honking as he finally guns in front of one of them. This process will repeat itself shortly, when the time comes to turn left, toward Sagg Beach.

When Stepfather's driving finally elicits a quiet complaint from the boy's mother, Stepfather redirects his road rage to the minivan's interior.

"Jesus, Sissy, don't be a backseat driver. You wonder why I don't let you drive? You need to be more aggressive." Stepfather's eyes meet the boy's in the rear-view mirror, his contradiction apparently unnoticed. "Dominic, dammit, move your head, I can't see out the back!" The boy shrinks into the backseat, dutifully ducking, gripping the cooler as Stepfather swerves again.

There are many other beaches along the same shoreline, many easier to access by car, but Sagg Beach is the only option. It is Stepfather's childhood beach, a short bike ride from his old family home. The girls sway against their seatbelts, laughing as the minivan flies past Ocean Road, the turn to the old homestead, oblivious. The boy grits his teeth and tightens his grip on the cooler, hoping his sandwich won't be crushed by a shifting soda can as he twists in his seat, trying to catch a glimpse of the old house.

The boy yearns for the thick, towering hedges that bordered Grandma and Grandpa's quiet, private yard, the tunnels and piney alcoves that seemed deliberately carved, perhaps by hobbits of the Shire or even elves from Rivendell, inviting the boy to recline on the soft, loamy earth and look up through the evergreens, through the diffuse light, and daydream, unnoticed, for hours at a time. He misses building cities out of oyster shells and pebbles in the driveway, marching his lead soldiers down long, winding avenues created by the tips of his fingers. He misses the particular mustiness inside, the salty air that had infused the house since it was built, in 1745, so unimaginably long ago. He misses its wide creaking boards, its dark back stairwell with its worn, silky rope handrail, the wavy plaster walls the boy used to find faces in. He misses Grandpa's asparagus patch.

The week passes quickly. There are no new lead soldiers for the boy's collection. Grandpa would have been disappointed.

The boy will remember those picnic lunches, clumps of tuna clinging to soggy bread, tearing off and falling onto the sandy blanket. He will remember picking up those wet, malleable balls of chunked fish and plopping them straight into his mouth, more willing to chew sand than invite Stepfather's criticism for wasting food.

He will remember wondering why vacation no longer improved Stepfather's mood as effectively as it always had in previous summers.

He will wonder whether it was simply the new brevity, a single week of play after decades of whole summers stretching back to his own childhood. He will wonder whether it was the loss of Stepfather's childhood home. He will wonder whether it was Grandpa's recent death.

The boy will remember throwing himself into the surf, angling his body against the roughest waves, allowing himself to be slammed to the ocean floor again and again, the current whisking him down the beach, a quarter mile at a time, until his family's blue-and-yellow-striped umbrella became a barely discernible dot on the horizon.

Perhaps it was the boy himself. His very presence, swaying and ducking in and out of the rear-view mirror, no longer an accepted guest.

SOCIAL STUDIES

THE BOY WILL SOON begin his sophomore year of high school, and he thinks, perhaps, that he is in love. Her name is Heather, and she has been a friend for some time, a close platonic companion through his freshman year. Suddenly she is more, a development that begins with an unexpected kiss shortly after the end of the school year.

The boy has never found Heather physically attractive. He has never objectified her as he does everyone else he regularly encounters, girls and boys alike, never even registered the possibility. He enjoys Heather for her company, her quick, sarcastic wit, her easily elicited, high-pitched, machine-gun laugh, her ready willingness to traipse all over town with the boy when he sneaks out after dark. They walk and talk while pursuing illicit little adventures in the night, arranging garden gnomes in provocative positions on a teacher's lawn or sneaking into the country club for a midnight swim. Often their planned adventures go forgotten, lost in a constant stream of easy banter, a totally new experience for the boy.

Much of their talk is devoted to their classmates, other boys and girls they objectify together, for each other, mercilessly dissecting their flaws while presenting options for each other's pursuit, if only either of them had the courage to act.

But that kiss, the boy's first that feels truly significant, puts an end to all that.

"I want you," Heather says, holding his cheeks in her hands, forcing direct eye contact, her words astonishingly succinct.

Everything changes, the boy thinks, uneasy and not understanding why.

"I want you," Heather repeats in the same earnest, searching tone. The boy closes his eyes and returns her kiss, preventing further words.

Since that first kiss, they've been inseparable. At the end of the school year, Stepfather arranges a summer job for the boy, pulling weeds and doing chores at an organic vegetable farm. Work begins at seven each morning, and the farm itself is nearly seven miles from home. It's hard work after a hard bike ride, upsy the whole way, but the boy no longer cares. He's long since stopped showing up, happily sacrificing his three-dollars-per-hour to spend his days with Heather, swimming at the lake, searching out hidden places where they might spend a few hours alone, or lazily passing the day in front of the television at Heather's home. The boy is perfectly aware that it's only a matter of time until Stepfather discovers his truancy. He pushes the thought away, ignoring the constant worry. He has mastered the art of compartmentalization, expertly parsing reality to suit his immediate desires.

Heather lives around the corner from the boy, at the end of a recently developed cul-de-sac cutting through what used to be uninterrupted marshland. The boy soon learns this development is Litchfield's reluctant effort to provide local workers with affordable housing. Heather lives in a two-story condo with her mother and younger sister. Sometimes they're joined by a man to whom Heather alternately refers as Dad or by his first name, Mark.

Mark is a compact, heavily muscled and tattooed man with a poorly repaired cleft palate, resulting in a prominent harelip and a lisp that the boy finds endearing, as well as a stern, difficult-to-read demeanor that, coupled with his intimidating stature, the boy finds slightly scary. When Mark arrives, usually in the evening, he often discovers the boy and Heather snuggling on the couch in front of the television.

"What're you ttthoo lovebirdths up tthoo?" he asks.

"Nothing, Mark," Heather replies, and sometimes, "Shut up, Dad!" The boy, always careful to gauge the moods of those around him and respond accordingly, has no idea how to read their dynamic. He subtly straightens on the couch, putting some distance between himself and Heather, waiting for some clue.

Heather's mother, Sheryl, is a nurse whose shifts begin in the middle of the night. She generally returns home around noon and immediately takes her reserved seat at the kitchen table, from which she can survey the living room and anyone in it, the television on should she find herself alone. She drinks tall cans of Budweiser while smoking full-flavored Marlboro 100s one after the other, recounting the horrors she encountered at the hospital to whomever will listen before retiring to bed while the sun is still high, attempting a few hours' sleep before resuming her routine. Grandpa, whose greatest joy was found in discovering strangers as willing to chat as he was, would have called Sheryl a "conversationalist of the highest order."

Sheryl will happily talk to whoever's handy, but she seems partial to the boy's company. The feeling is mutual. The boy has never encountered an adult to whom he can speak without carefully minding his words, although he avoids discussing his family too deeply. Despite that, or more likely because of his obvious omission, Sheryl intuitively understands that he is not comfortable at home. She doesn't seem to mind his constant presence. In fact, she feigns annoyance when he arrives later than usual.

"You're about as reliable as a used condom, Dominic," she scolds through a cloud of smoke, gesturing with her long cigarette. "My daughter's been pining away in her room all day. Pining, I tell you! Now grab me a beer and sit down and talk to me, she'll wait a little longer. You know you're always welcome here, right?"

The boy takes full advantage of Sheryl's open invitation. Most days, he lies to his mother, calling to inform her that he'll be spending the night at some familiar male friend's house.

"So whose house are we staying at tonight, Dominic?" Sheryl asks, chuckling as the boy hangs up the phone. "Can't be this skid row dump! Mrs. Marshall wouldn't like that, would she? Oh no!"

"Are you sure you don't mind if I stay?" the boy always asks.

"Of course not, honey, we love having you here. How many times do I have to tell you? The high-and-mighty Marshalls' loss is our gain! Grab me another beer while you're up, will you? You guys want pizza or Chinese tonight? I'm feeling rich, take advantage!"

On nights when his mother insists that he come home, the boy returns for dinner and uses his supposed job as an excuse to go to bed early. He lies awake in his loft bed in his basement room, the guest bedroom when his grandparents still owned the house, fully clothed and shoed, listening to the sounds of the family above as they prepare for their own beds.

As soon as the house is quiet, he sneaks out through the casement window above his bed, creeping across the backyard, mounting his bike and silently coasting down the dark street, returning to Heather's condo in little more than a minute. The job, if he were still working it, starts early enough that he won't be missed in the morning. He buries the fear that Stepfather might discover his absence during the night, another successful manipulation of his reality.

He sleeps soundly, well into the morning in Heather's comfortable little bed, while Sheryl is still at work.

But before sleeping, the boy has silent, self-conscious sex with Heather in five-minute intervals. He pulls out just before ejaculating and immediately enters her again for another five minutes, a race to repeat, always in the dark, always in the same missionary position, frantically thrusting away, his eyes squeezed shut, his hands clutching the pillow behind her head, his face buried in her hair.

This act the boy remains unable to compartmentalize.

Shortly into the beginning of his sophomore year, Heather breaks up with the boy. It happens suddenly, over the phone, a totally unexpected turn to a conversation simply meant to arrange a date for later the same day. Heather tearfully tells the boy that she doesn't want to see him anymore. He demands to know why. Heather hangs up. He calls back. He repeats the process twice, more frantic with each hang up.

On his fourth call, Sheryl answers. In an unrecognizably hard voice, she cuts off the boy's confused pleading with the words, "I think you've done quite enough. Don't call here again. Leave my daughter alone." A click, and a dial tone.

The boy will never forget Stepfather's words when he finally learned where the boy had spent all his time that summer. Although Stepfather didn't make his discovery until later in the fall, weeks after Heather had already ended the relationship, it was during that lecture that it was decided that the boy should leave the family and move in with his father as soon as possible.

"If the boy wants to waste his days rutting away in some low-rent condo, he should do just fine in Maryland," Stepfather declares to the boy's mother. And despite the boy's repeated assurances that his relationship with Heather had ended, Stepfather turns to the boy and says, "But if you get that girl pregnant, Dominic, don't even think of coming to us for help. I got you that job for a reason, and you blew it. You bring nothing but shame to this family."

You bring nothing but shame to this family. That phrase in particular, so heavy with formality, will haunt the boy.

He will wonder whether it was his constant presence in Heather's home, using her to escape his own, suffocating her, monopolizing conversation with her mother. He will wonder whether it was his inadequate sexual performance, his inability to enjoy the experience, to enjoy her, to give enjoyment in return. He will wonder whether he impregnated her with his joyless, silent thrusting. He will never know.

In the future, the man this boy is to become will remain somewhat frigid with his sexual partners, all the way through his twenties, and premature ejaculation will remain a constant frustration for both them and him. After all, Stepfather trained him to want to end sex as quickly as possible. Stepfather taught him not to want sex at all.

Stepfather taught him shame, and he learned his lesson well.

THE BOY WITH THE
PURPLE CRAYON

THE BOY MISSES HEATHER, especially when they pass each other in the halls between classes and she deliberately avoids his eyes. He feels as if they should simply acknowledge the awkwardness between them, find a way to laugh at each other as they would have laughed at anyone else's acting so stupidly a few months ago.

"Aren't we ridiculous? Aren't we just hilarious?" they'd mock, immediately getting back to the business of being friends, as easy together as they had once been.

But Heather obviously isn't interested in speaking, let alone joking with him. He wishes he could be Harold, the boy with the purple crayon, as he had so often imagined as a younger child. He would erase that kiss and all that came after. He would draw a new history, defined by simple purple lines.

Instead, he ratchets up his running habit, although he's traded the cross-country team for rowing with the school crew. The boy falls in love with rowing fast and hard. When he isn't rowing, he runs, and as he runs he thinks about rowing, eager for the next opportunity to lace his feet into the boat's stationary shoes and prop himself on its hard, sliding seat, to still his body to perfect posture in the narrow skull, barely wider than his hips, to see the lake passing under the translucent membrane of the boat's thin fiberglass shell, his hands reaching out beyond the gunwales, shoveling great scoops of water with his oar, a twelve-foot-long extension of his arms. *Go, go, gadget arm*, he thinks, again and again, in perfect time with each stroke, all extraneous thought thoroughly, beautifully expelled from his mind.

The crew gets out on the water every school day at dawn and again in the afternoon. They often practice over the weekend as well, preparing for spring competition with larger prep school crews, with their superior equipment, their rabidly devoted alumni, their limitless funds, their rivalries rivaling Texas football. The schedule suits the boy's needs perfectly. That fall, he rarely finds it necessary to create excuses to be away from home.

Between practices, whether in class, pounding pavement in his running shoes, or avoiding Stepfather in the bathroom, the boy visualizes his body poised a few inches above the lake's surface, serene and glassy in the morning, dark and choppy later in the day, stroking his long oar through the water with carefully controlled strength, matching the cadence of the coxswain's call, pulling harder, stronger, more smoothly, deliberately directing power out of his body as it extends and curls down and up the sliding seat, radiating from his flexing legs and accordion core, out through his back and down his arms, his oar like a great gadget wing, all while keeping the pace controlled, consistent, as balanced as the long, slim boat itself.

Surely, the boy thinks, this newfound control, this suddenly discovered strength, can be translated into overcoming his fear of Stepfather. At the very least, he should be able to channel this kinetic energy into his own escape. He visualizes a sharp knife sluicing through all resistance, directed by nothing more than his mind, the constant danger of capsizing prevented only by the boy's metronomic precision. *Go, go, gadget boat*, his mantra changes in the moment when he can no longer distinguish his body's movement from the boat's forward motion, cutting the water in a perfectly straight line.

He shows quick talent for the sport's required rhythm, and the coach informs the boy that he will stroke the varsity boat during the spring regatta season. He will sit the sternmost seat, the captain's position, and set the pace for the rowers stretching to the bow behind him, sometimes three, sometimes seven, depending on the race, all juniors and seniors, all reacting to the boy's subtlest motion. He has never known such pride.

The crew draws its members from two schools in addition to the boy's, including the school where his mother and Stepfather still teach, all pooling resources to provide this expensive sport for their students. The boy fills Heather's absence with new friends from other schools, older boys and girls who take pleasure in teaching their sophomore captain how to smoke pot and shotgun beers in the woods behind the boathouse, skills at which they can display superior talent to the boy's.

The boy learns these new, faster paths to oblivion eagerly. His extracurricular runs become shorter, now just a means to get himself to the woods, where he can smoke pot in solitude, losing himself in stillness, his carefully curated running soundtrack pounding out of his headphones, music that once propelled him forward mile after mile, newly appreciated as he sits and smokes and observes his anxieties from a comfortable distance.

Shortly before the fall practice breaks for winter, the boy meets someone who expresses unabashed interest in him. As with Heather, he's not sure that he's particularly attracted to her. But he seems to be as incapable of rejecting anyone who expresses interest in him as he is of expressing his own interest in others. Besides, she is entirely new to the boy. This time, there is no history of friendship to jeopardize.

Her name is Sam, and she is nineteen, a young woman spending a postgraduate year at yet another nearby prep school, attempting to polish her high school transcript in preparation for Ivy League applications. Sam commutes to school from her mother's home in Litchfield, as near the boy's home as Heather's, in the exact opposite direction.

The boy quickly falls into a similar routine with Sam as he had with Heather, sneaking out through his basement window as often as possible and spending the night in Sam's luxurious bedroom, with its posted bed and separate sitting area, its ensuite bathroom and magically refreshed supply of monogrammed towels, evidence of a cleaning lady's labor the boy never observes.

On the weekends, they sleep well into the day in an undisturbed cocoon of sex-stained cotton sheets, the room dark behind blackout curtains. During the week, the couple shares hazelnut-flavored coffee and buttery croissants with Sam's mother in the morning. *How fucking civilized*, the boy thinks, never voicing the thought even to Sam, never entirely comfortable in her well-appointed, perfectly maintained home.

Sam's mother is divorced from her doctor father, who is rarely mentioned by either Sam or her mother. Sam's grandmother lives in the in-law apartment above the garage. Sometimes she joins them for coffee and croissants before heading off to volunteer at the library or the historical society, common venues at which she often encounters the boy's own grandmother. *Beware the hysterical society,* the boy thinks, unable to avoid Stepfather's voice in his head, his parting words to his own mother whenever she volunteers at the little town museum. *Don't bring any hysterics home!*

Neither of Sam's elders seem bothered by the boy's constant presence any more than Heather's mother had, although their demeanors are as opposite as their homes. No matter the hour, Sam's mother and grandmother never fail to present patrician manners, a stark contrast to Sheryl's husky smoker's chuckle and daytime Budweisers. While Sheryl lived in her nurse's scrubs, Sam's mother and grandmother are perfectly dressed by dawn. Their home could engulf four of Sheryl's condo. Despite these differences, the boy finds similarities in sentiment between his new girlfriend's household and Heather's.

"We enjoy a touch of testosterone in the house, don't we, girls?" Sam's mother often asks, winking at the boy as she refills his mug with pungent coffee. The boy finds the hot hazelnut aroma nauseating but dutifully sips.

"That we do!" Sam's grandmother replies. "Dominic, I always tell your grandmother how much I envy her such a fine grandson. Not that we don't adore our Sam, you understand. But the yard work! You're always welcome, dear, especially if I can convince you to pick up a snow shovel now and then."

"I'm happy to shovel anytime, Mrs. Wolcott," the boy assures her.

"I always enjoy a touch of your testosterone," Sam whispers in the boy's ear, brazenly squeezing his crotch under the kitchen table. The boy shifts in his seat, burying his blush in his mug of nutty coffee.

Sam drops the boy off at school in her stick-shift Subaru before heading off to her own classes for the day. The boy likes it that Sam drives a completely unremarkable standard sedan when she could have a BMW, like her mother, or at least a Volvo, like her grandmother. He likes her for insisting on the boyish abbreviation of her full name, *Samantha*, so very WASPy. Sometimes he wonders why he feels the need to consciously check off the qualities he likes in his new girlfriend.

As Sam pulls up in front of his school, the boy leans over for a quick kiss goodbye. She responds by grabbing his crotch again as she messily inserts her tongue in his mouth, always insatiable. Some days, they abruptly decide to skip school altogether, searching out a private place to park and smoke pot and listen to the Chemical Brothers while having especially awkward sex in the car. They never talk too deeply, at least not the way he used to with Heather. Sam doesn't seem to mind the boy's lack of sexual confidence any more than she minds their age difference, and as a result, the boy has become slightly more confident. He likes her for that, too. Check.

For the first time, the boy has earned status among his peers at school. Suddenly, he attracts notice from people he's never spoken to. He overhears their whispers, the unavoidable rumors of a tiny, insulated campus:

Did you hear that he's captain of the crew? Is he even old enough to drive? I mean, he's just a sophomore. Is that his girlfriend dropping him off? What's her name? Samantha? She's a Wolcott, right? Didn't she go to Taft? Isn't she in college? Didn't he used to date that Heather girl? Doesn't she live in the condos? Wow, he really moved up. I hear he knows how to get pot. We should totally invite them to your party next weekend.

The boy separates his disgust from his pride, eliminating his discomfort as effectively as a sneeze dispels the nausea that came before. He gives himself over to enjoying his newfound status, his newly acquired recognition, so foreign to the boy's young experience. He will captain the boat. He will attend the parties. He will shotgun the beers. He will procure the pot. He will endure the hazelnut coffee. He will fuck his older, wealthier, *better* girlfriend, whether he likes her or not.

He will become Harold, drawing a new history with his purple crayon.

SHAME AND SENSIBILITIES

FEBRUARY 1994 CARRIES a flavor that the boy will recall with particular clarity in the years to come, a distinct aroma associated with the dark, cold winter evenings of that month, every day blanketed under a shower of new, wet snow, contrasting with the warm, dry interior of Sam's car or bedroom. Anticipation. Change. Fear. Freedom. The funky smells of pot, sex, and hazelnut coffee all mixed together, somehow not entirely unpleasant.

Without fail, he is always doing something wrong—or more accurately, something Stepfather would not approve of. The boy balances on an edge as narrow and tipsy as his beloved rowing skulls, inviting punishment with his easily exposed lies, thin deceptions hiding his whereabouts and ever more illicit adventures, a clichéd combination of sex, drugs, and hard-hitting electronic beats that he seeks with myopic purpose, narrowly focused on each moment before him.

He isn't beyond caring, exactly. He dreads Stepfather's discovery, the certain consequences that will follow. But he ignores that fear, shifting it beyond the scope of his vision as easily as Sam's car shifts from fourth to fifth gear, accelerating, leaving something unnameable behind, desperately seeking oblivion, escape.

He will turn sixteen in two weeks, a meaningless milestone as far as the boy is concerned. That day, nothing will change except that he will be one day closer to moving to Maryland, to moving in with his father, his *real* Dad, to a new life with a new family. To a life without Stepfather.

In the meantime, Sam lavishes attention on the boy, demanding his in return.

"We've got four months left together, and I intend to make the most of it," she assures the boy, her tone uncomfortably close to Stepfather's "pack it in" mania before those dreaded Hampton vacations of recent years. Sam arranges exotic dinners out: Cantonese, Indian, and Japanese steak houses. Her mother prepares special dinners in: lobster, fondue, and prime rib. There are parties to attend.

This weekend's party is hosted by one of Sam's college friends who found herself alone with her parents' house for a few days. After smoking pot, a brief bout of sweaty sex, and a twenty-minute drive, Sam pulls her Subaru into a secluded driveway, its wrought iron gate thrown open between stone pillars. The winding, tree-lined driveway is festively illuminated, sparkling white Christmas lights draping every tree, pointing the way to a columned, glowing colonial mansion, its wings spreading out into darkness.

A man—*a fucking butler?* the boy wonders—waves as Sam pulls her car to the front of the house. The butler sports a newsboy cap instead of a bowler and his gloves are black instead of white, yet he wouldn't be out of place in that BBC production of *Pride and Prejudice* the boy's mother and sisters love so much. The boy has no doubt that his accent will be English.

The butler, *Mister Bingley*, as the boy immediately fixates upon him, wears his long, formal black coat with perfect ease, its wide lapels flipped up, shielding his ears, a snow-white scarf framing his jaw. *Why, Mister Bingley, sir, don't we cut a fine figure*, the boy thinks. The butler holds up one hand and points at the ground before his feet with the other, instructing Sam where to stop.

The boy recalls spending the rare evening in the family room, down in the basement just outside his own bedroom, gathered in front of the television with his mother and sisters while Stepfather was out working or making music.

He remembers the actress who played Jane's mother in *Pride and Prejudice*, her exaggerated accent giving "Mister Bingley" those particular emphases, her distinct exclamation at the end of each syllable, title, and name, *Mister Bingley*. He remembers his mother, her voice parroting that actress perfectly, calling the boy *Mister Bingley* at every opportunity for weeks after, dictating his perception of all English accents forever. The boy feels pleased with the unexpected opportunity to assign his mother's slightly annoying moniker to someone perhaps better suited to the role.

Where are all the cars, Mister Bingley? the boy wonders at the butler, his pot-heavy brain not overly concerned. Still, he can't avoid a twinge of anxiety. He's never been entirely comfortable in Sam's house, with its unseen daily maid, let alone a home equipped with valet parking. *This is no kid's party, is it, Mister Bingley?* he silently asks.

Sam leaps from the car without hesitation, leaving her door ajar and the car running. The boy slowly follows.

"Thank you," he says to Mister Bingley, who nods but doesn't respond, just waves them toward the house as he climbs behind the Subaru's wheel. The boy is disappointed. *Won't you send us on with a word, Mister Bingley?* He'd hoped to verify that accent.

Muffled music, voices, and laughter drift on the cold air, emanating from the house, suddenly more distinct as an upstairs window opens.

"Sam, is that you?" a featureless silhouette calls from the window.

"Yes, darling!" Sam yells back, waving, and the boy abruptly despises her. *Darling.* Her tone is so contrived, trying so hard to mimic her rich divorcee mother and hysterical society grandmother. The boy could swear he smells hazelnut, curdling his stomach. He stifles a sudden urge to sneeze, allowing his nausea to linger.

"Come straight upstairs!" the unseen *darling* yells. The window slams shut, the party instantly muted.

The boy follows Sam through the front doors, two of them, glossy black, tall and wide, *like Saint John's cathedral,* the boy thinks, forcing himself not to ogle. Inside, the foyer displays dark Victorian furniture, bright modern art, thick Persian rugs, everything arranged just so but for the empty beer bottles and plastic cups littering every surface. *We'll have our work cut out for us tomorrow, won't we, Mister Bingley?* the boy thinks.

A wide staircase climbs two floors above. To the left and right are rooms filled with people, standing and swaying to drum and bass coming from somewhere deeper inside. Someone yells a greeting at Sam. She waves, then takes the boy by the hand and pulls him along as she bounds up the stairs, two at a time.

At the second floor landing, the boy observes a couple reclining in a window seat overlooking the dark backyard. Snow-covered tennis courts and a tarped pool are briefly illuminated by sweeping headlights, Mister Bingley parking Sam's Subaru somewhere out of sight. The young woman reclining against the windowsill appears barely conscious, her head supported only by her shoulder. The young man next to her has his hand up her short plaid skirt. He looks up and registers Sam.

"Oh, hey, Sam," he says, so casual, but Sam ignores him, dragging the boy away, down the hall, past more modern art and black-framed sepia photographs, toward *darling*'s room. The boy looks back at the young woman in the window. She lazily swats her suitor's hand away, her head still lolling to the side, her eyes closed.

Sam opens a door onto a sitting room fully outfitted with television, stereo, a couch, and papasan chairs, pulling the boy in behind her. The sitting room is unoccupied, but a cloud of smog drifts from the hallway beyond, a galley kitchenette complete with sink, dormitory refrigerator, and microwave, the counters and shelves littered with beer cans and empty wine bottles, directing them toward the bedroom beyond.

Six girls sit on the bedroom floor around a glass bong and a pale blue china soup bowl filled with white powder propping up a silver teaspoon. Playing cards are strewn across the floor, and the girls are in varying stages of undress. One of the girls, wearing only panties and a Nirvana *Unplugged* T-shirt, surges to her feet and leaps at Sam, wrapping her arms and one long, bare leg around her. They kiss, lingering on each other's lips, giggling, spinning around, not caring when they knock over the bong. Foul water spills onto the carpet, soaking some of the cards. The seated girls protest. Sam and Darling ignore them.

"Finally!" Darling says through her kissing lips. Slowly separating herself from Sam, she turns her attention to the boy. "So this is him."

"This is Dominic," the boy says, sticking out his hand. Darling reflexively offers her own, and without pause the boy raises her hand to his mouth and kisses it, pleased and shocked by his sudden temerity. Darling also appears pleased. She introduces herself, but the boy immediately forgets her name. He will only ever remember her as Darling.

Darling, apparently charmed by the boy, invites him to participate in her girls-only strip poker tournament, which is "just getting interesting," she assures him. While Sam refills the bong in the kitchenette sink, Darling takes the boy by the hand and guides him to the floor, seating herself next to him, leaving no room for Sam, who is forced to squeeze in across the circle. Sam has never expressed jealousy before, another noted check in the boy's "like" column, but the boy, always sensitive, detects that she's slightly uncomfortable with the seating arrangement. He tries to maintain a few inches of space between his crossed legs and Darling's, but Darling leans against him every time she laughs, loudly and often. *Why, Mister Bingley, what's this situation we find ourselves in?* the boy thinks.

The group passes the bong around the circle continuously while playing some version of poker the boy can't follow and continuing to remove clothing. Darling scoops a heaping teaspoon of cocaine onto a small silver tray and offers it to the boy. He has only recently been introduced to this higher form of oblivion and has never seen so much of it gathered in one place before. Unwilling to expose his naivety by asking directions, the boy takes the glass straw Darling offers and cuts straight through the pile in one huge snort.

"Wow, rock star!" Darling exclaims, giggling and wrapping her arm around his waist. She kisses the boy on the cheek, then looks across the circle at Sam. "Fun *and* cute! Can I play with him?" Sam smiles and nods, taking her own snort, waving at Darling to do as she will as she sniffles, her eyes wide.

Darling loses the next hand and insists that the boy help her out of her shirt, then her bra. Only her panties remain, and the boy carefully averts his eyes. Laughing, Darling takes his hand and guides it to her breast, squeezing her hand over the boy's. He feels her nipple harden against his palm.

"It's okay, Sam doesn't mind. We're *very* close. Aren't we, Sam?" Sam doesn't appear to have heard, manically chatting with the other girls across the circle, but she can plainly see what's happening. The boy assumes she would say something, or at least give some indication if she were upset. Through suddenly roaring ears, the boy hears Darling saying something about too many clothes and fairness and being a gentleman. The boy realizes that she wants him to take off his own clothes.

"Not *fair*," she says again, tugging at the waist of his jeans. The boy finds words spilling from his mouth, something about Mister Bingley and a gentleman never making a lady uncomfortable, and as Darling pulls him to his feet and begins fumbling with his belt, the boy wonders whether he's talking too much or too fast or both. *What the hell are we doing here, Mister Bingley?* he asks himself.

He has never been so high. Through the onslaught of cocaine coursing through his ears, through his weirdly crystalized eyes, through the distinct awareness of his every hair follicle, his too-fast, too-many thoughts, his anxiety heightened yet slipping away concurrently, the boy suddenly realizes that he is about to get naked in a roomful of girls. His long-recurring nightmare, the awful dream that began back in Kathy's kitchen, so long ago. The boy is shocked to find himself unafraid. In fact, eagerly the opposite. He smiles at Darling, suddenly desperately attracted to her.

With Darling's help, he strips. He even tries to make it sexy, in a gawky, never-dances-or-even-dreams-of-performing sort of way. Despite (or perhaps because of) his lack of grace, Darling and the rest of the girls laugh and hoot, including Sam, encouraging him as first his sweater comes off, then his shoes, his jeans, his shirt, his socks, Darling pulling each item from his body with a flourish before tossing them to the circle. The girls grab for his flying clothes, urging him on.

When only his boxers remain, Darling takes the boy by his shoulders and pushes him down onto her huge bed, landing on top of him, straddling his body, grinding against his strangely shameless erection. Led by Sam, the rest of the girls follow, leaving the poker game behind and joining Darling and the boy, laughing and touching him. Darling leans close, her breasts mashed against his chest. She reaches between her legs and his, stroking him through his boxers, whispering in his ear, "I want a look at this."

Through his roaring thoughts, the boy feels himself drift. He stretches his arms above his head, allowing his body to go limp. Darling shimmies his boxers down his legs and off his feet, tossing them over her shoulder, climbing back on him, kissing his neck and rubbing against the length of his body. The boy is aware of Sam, kneeling behind Darling, nearly naked now herself, pressing against Darling's back, kissing the nape of her neck.

For a brief moment, Sam's eyes meet the boy's. She smiles. The boy relaxes further, surrendering but not overtly participating. He locks his hands above his head and schools his body to stillness. He feels an odd, unfamiliar sense of control. When Darling takes him in her mouth for a moment, he laughs with pleasure but resists the urge to thrust, distinctly aware that he had been inside Sam little more than an hour earlier. Seemingly unconcerned, Sam kisses him. The boy returns her kiss with passion he has never felt for her.

The other girls, annoyed or perhaps uncomfortable with the party's sudden turn, demand that the threesome untangle themselves and return to the game. Astonished to hear his own words, the boy demands a new game. He wants a bath. The girls will wash Sam off of him. Perhaps he will feel more free once the evidence of her sex is gone from his skin.

The girls oblige, laughing as they half drag, half carry his naked body through a huge closet into a bathroom the size of the boy's own bedroom. The girls make a great show of pouring his bath, adding bubbles, testing the temperature, finally sinking him into the tub. Darling steps out of her panties and climbs in behind him, folding her long legs over his, fondling him under the water and nibbling on his ear. The boy is hyperaware of her pubic hair rubbing against the small of his back as she flexes her legs against his. The other girls, including Sam, take turns shampooing his hair and soaping his chest.

Eventually tiring of the game, the other girls return to their cocaine and pot in the bedroom, leaving the boy alone with Darling and Sam. Darling abruptly declares that the boy needs a good grooming and proceeds to do just that. She begins innocently enough, plucking the boy's eyebrows and stray hairs from his ears, his nose. The boy feels nothing but pleasure and excitement. Sam assists from the bathtub's edge, obeying Darling's direction.

When Darling tells the boy to stand, pointing at his crotch with a

79

small pair of scissors and remarking that he needs trimmed before she'll fuck him, Sam's jealousy finally reveals itself.

"Please don't, darling? He's *my* boyfriend, after all," she says. Her pleading tone combined with that contrived patrician address brings the boy's earlier flash of disgust for her back all at once.

"Well of course he is!" Darling replies, immediately climbing from the tub. "But you did say I could play with him, *darling*. Let's all take a shower together and get back to the party. Looks like your *boyfriend* could use a cold one."

Play with Darling doesn't stop with the shower. Despite Sam's earlier protest, she makes no comment as Darling runs the water hot, soaping the boy up, lingering on his crotch, rubbing her own sudsy body against the boy's. He will remember his passivity, his tacit agreement, his lack of concern for Sam.

After the shower, on Darling's dare, the boy walks through the house naked. He strolls down the stairs, through the rest of the party, to the kitchen, nodding to those who look at him as they part to make way, shocked, disgusted, perhaps even afraid. Unconcerned, the boy politely bids them "good evening" in his best imitation of his mother's Mister Bingley voice. He grabs a beer from the refrigerator. Slowly, deliberately, he opens the beer, takes a long swig, and walks back up the stairs to Darling's room, basking in this new, strange sense of control, his fear of nudity conquered. He will never dream of public exposure again.

The boy sleeps in Darling's bed that night, nestled naked between her and Sam, their bodies pressing against his. He lies awake long after they sleep, aware of the tension between them.

Eventually, the boy sleeps. As usual, he wakes with the dawn and discovers that he turned to Darling instead of Sam during the night. He regretfully moves away from Darling's naked body, careful not to disturb either of his bedmates, adjusting himself to straight stillness, flat on his back, hands chastely crossed on his chest, willing his morning erection to disappear, Stepfather's words rattling through the boy's thoughts, *you bring nothing but shame to this family.*

DISTANCE = RATE × TIME

HE MOVES FROM Connecticut to Cumberland on the train immediately after the end of his sophomore year. It's the second week of June. He's visited his father several times since that first meeting, but this is it. The final move. Clothes, books, music, even his most prized possession, an Aiwa bookshelf stereo with detachable speakers, bulky but essential, are all packed into a huge, handed-down suitcase and three heavy duffels.

Shortly after dawn on the day after the school year concludes, a hired driver packs the boy into a Town Car. The limo, a gift chartered by his Tough Cookie grandmother, will deliver the boy to New Haven's Amtrak terminus. From there he will travel by train through New York and Philadelphia to Baltimore, where his father will collect the boy for the final drive to Cumberland.

The boy's mother looks on, barely restraining her tears. Her fear of driving has grown into terror in recent years. She will no longer drive anywhere near a city, and Stepfather certainly isn't going to assist the boy's desertion. As far as the boy is concerned, that's just fine.

So he travels comfortably, until arriving at the train station at least. Previous trips had familiarized the boy with the New Haven terminus. Normally he'd buy a cup of coffee, smoke a cigarette on the street, pretend to be much older than his sixteen years, and just feel his freedom while waiting for the train. This time, he's burdened with too much luggage and can't risk leaving it unattended. He regrets the lost opportunity, but only briefly.

It begins to sink in. He is *out*. Out of Stepfather's reach, out of that house, and out of that picture-perfect little Connecticut town, where every landmark is a reminder of misery. The boy's life is suddenly, all at once, his own.

The boy imagines that he may never experience that morning's particular sense of endless freedom stretching before him again, but he will recall it as perfectly as he'll always recall the taste and aroma of Jack Daniels Tennessee Whiskey. That moment will forever stand alone in the boy's mind, its flavor the polar opposite of sour: shockingly, overwhelmingly sweet.

And then he arrives in Baltimore.

On recent visits to his Maryland family, as the boy delineates them, he would take the train to Washington, DC, where he would change trains at Union Station, traveling on his own all the way west to Cumberland. This time there's a significant difference in price if he disembarks in Baltimore. The new itinerary also allows the boy to avoid the hassle of transferring so much luggage between trains, and it shortens the overall trip by a few hours, so he doesn't mind. Until he sees the place.

The boy has never been to Baltimore, and DC's Union Station is not exactly representative of train stations elsewhere. It doubles as a bustling shopping mall and Metro stop little more than a block from the Capitol. Generally, the boy would layover there for a couple of hours. He'd get a big slice of pizza at Sbarro, treat himself to a new book, and find a place where he could alternate between reading and people-watching near the reflecting pool until the time came to board.

New Haven's train station is not particularly lovely, but it's small and feels relatively safe. The boy does not feel safe in Baltimore, although the station's architecture is similar to New Haven's in both size and style. There are lots of vagrants and few cops, none of whom meet the boy's eyes as he shuffles past, smiling uncertainly. The boy makes an easy target with all his luggage, obviously displaced, and he feels all the wrong eyes following him everywhere he goes. And he does go everywhere, searching for his father, who is nowhere to be found.

The boy waits for two hours as his bladder becomes uncomfortably distended. He finds no easily accessible restrooms in his brief survey of the station. He berates himself for not using the train's facilities while he had the chance. He'd intended to, but by the time he felt the need he'd become worried about missing his new, unfamiliar stop. In the third hour, still waiting, the situation has become dire. Every movement he makes disturbs the distended water balloon his bladder feels like, risking rupture.

The boy's luggage limits his options. The suitcase, at least, certainly won't fit in a locker. The boy seriously considers allowing himself to simply piss his pants but quickly concludes that he is not quite cowardly enough for that extreme. It's been years since he's wet himself in his sleep, a victory he can't imagine surrendering while conscious. He begins another circuit of the station.

He discovers restroom signs pointing down a short flight of stairs in one of the station's secluded corners. Several men are sprawled on the floor of the downstairs landing, sleeping, forcing the boy to exercise extreme strength as he shoulders his bags and hoists his suitcase high, adding pressure to his bladder and somehow absorbing it, carefully stepping around and over the bodies at his feet, terrified that he might disturb one of them, or worse, lose control of his barely restrained bladder over one of them, imagining the worst possible scenarios if he were to do so.

Finally, he arrives at the bathroom's threshold, sweating.

A man stands over one of the urinals with both hands on the wall. His pants are down, bunched around his ankles. A second man leans against his back, one hand braced against the wall, the other furiously working, shoving something into the first man's exposed ass. It looks like a length of black pipe. The man doing the shoving meets the boy's eyes as he absorbs the scene, stunned. The man withdraws whatever it is he's using to fuck the other man and turns toward the boy, chest heaving. Then the man takes a step toward the boy.

It was like last fall, after Heather broke up with him, when the boy had intended to run away. *Really* run away this time, finally ready to listen to that subversive voice always telling him to *just go*. That voice had recently become loud enough that the boy decided it needed a name. He settled on Gozer, as in Gozer the Gozerian, Gozer the Destructor, from *Ghostbusters*, of all things. Somehow Gozer, that evil spirit with his wolfish mastiffs in that silly movie, encompassed all the boy's most subversive thoughts at that age.

He hadn't yet been offered the option of moving to Maryland permanently, and without Heather's home to escape to, the boy had been unable to bear the thought of another year spent navigating Stepfather, the constant anxiety of avoiding him, lying to him, absorbing his punishments when he inevitably caught the boy in his lies. The boy saw another year of the same, constant burden, and another, with no end in sight. Gozer offered his only way out.

The boy planned his escape carefully, informing his mother that he would be visiting his father at Thanksgiving. The boy had no intention of traveling to Maryland, hadn't even discussed the possibility with his *real* Dad. He gathered what little money he could and bought a bus ticket to New York. He would stay in a hostel and seek work in a restaurant. It would be hard, but he would be fine, he was certain. He looked and felt much older than his age. He was ready.

When the boy arrived at Port Authority, fully resolved to call his mother and explain why he was never coming home, he was mugged at knife point. A young man, likely near the boy's own age, forced him back into the phone booth, the sharp end of his switchblade pressed against the boy's neck. In retrospect, the boy will recall that he easily outweighed his attacker. He could have wielded the phone receiver as a weapon and escaped, but the thought never even crossed his mind. He immediately gave up his meager belongings while urine soaked his pants.

The mugging left the boy utterly incapable of imagining himself on his own, thoroughly dispelling Gozer's subversive voice, that part of himself that so convincingly entertained dreams of freedom and independence every night. His plan disrupted, the boy finally called his father collect, abandoning Gozer's grand ideas and begging his *real* Dad to take him to safety.

His father immediately wired money for the boy to take the train to Cumberland. When the boy arrived the next day, he told his father an abbreviated and largely false version of that story. The boy had wanted to surprise his father, that was all, but it went horribly wrong.

His father's response surprised the boy. Instead of questioning or comforting or scolding him, his father focused strictly on the mugging. His father asked him to recite words that might prevent a repeat situation in the future. Words that now flooded the boy's mind, cynical instructions that he desperately hoped would apply.

"Hey, do you have a couple bucks?" the boy blurts. "I lost my wallet and I can't get home! I just need to make a phone call!"

The other man pulls up his pants, grabs his partner by the arm, and breathlessly says, "Let's get the fuck out of here." The boy cringes out of their way, brushing shoulders with each of them as they pass, nearly crying out in fear. His need to pee forgotten, the boy dumps his luggage to the floor and lurches toward the urinals and pukes in and around one of them, his breath coming in huge, hyperventilating gasps.

Finally, with nothing left to vomit, the boy manages to control his breathing. And then he urinates. Forever. He's so shaky he barely avoids pissing his pants after all and then barely manages to hit the urinal. He rinses his mouth and his hands and splashes his face. The wall-mounted dispensers contain no soap or towels. He leans over the sink, dripping, until his shaking subsides. Thankfully, no one else enters the bathroom. His luggage is safe.

When he finally manages to make it back through the sleeping bodies on the landing and up the stairs, the boy finds his father turning in circles in the middle of the station. His father's friend Kenny, a ruddy-faced, hugely tall and broad man perpetually smiling and smoking, stands with him, scanning the crowd, smiling wider and waving when he catches sight of the boy. The boy's father, partial to two-seater sports cars from the time he was old enough to drive, had apparently enlisted Kenny's help to haul the boy's luggage in his big SUV. The boy is grateful for Kenny's presence. He finds him much more approachable than the relative stranger he is now supposed to call *Dad*, much as the boy yearns to do so comfortably.

Kenny and his father relieve the boy of his luggage. They're quickly out of the station and into the SUV, a huge Toyota that reminds the boy of Litchfield soccer moms and instantly complicates his emotions. Is he already feeling homesick? Isn't this home now? Shouldn't he be happy? Is he not?

The incident he witnessed in the bathroom quickly takes on a surreal, unbelievable quality as Kenny's SUV merges onto the highway, speeding west toward Cumberland, the boy's final destination. Kenny lights a cigarette, cracks his window, and catches the boy's eye in the rearview mirror, smiling his constant smile.

"Hey, kid, there's a cooler behind your seat. Grab your old man and me a couple beers, will you? There's Coke for you."

The boy is shocked by the idea of someone so unabashedly intending to consume alcohol on a two-hour drive. *Is this why he was late? Were they drinking?* This is not something he's ever been exposed to, but he barely hesitates to do as instructed. *Can't be any worse than Stepfather's driving,* he thinks. The boy grabs two cans of Milwaukee's Best from the cooler and passes them up front. He skips the Coke and falls asleep almost immediately.

In the years to come, the boy will wonder whether his mother's growing fear of driving correlated with her ever-diminishing ability to shield the boy from Stepfather's ever-escalating rage. He will remember his mother standing in the driveway in the thin dawn light as the Town Car stood running, crying as the livery man loaded the boy's luggage, sadly waving as the limo pulled away, looking ancient and utterly defeated.

The boy will never tell his father what he witnessed in that bathroom. How could he name something so near his own secret? How could he bring that secret to his new life with his new family?

Best to bury it all down deep. Best to forget.

He will lose the next sixteen years trying to do just that.

II

MILLER

The Socratic Method

ORIENTATION

IMAGINE YOURSELF an observer, helplessly hypervigilant, constantly measuring your surroundings, never quite participating. Detached, considering, gauging. Watching.

Now your name is Miller. You're twenty-three years old, newly married and working a new job. Your first *real* job, according to your restaurateur father. After all, the sum of your experience to date was earned within the supposedly comfortable confines of the family business. There was room for only one manager in that situation, the position permanently occupied by your father.

But now you've become a restaurant manager in your own right, responsible for the dining room of a rather bougie hotel recently developed by the Disney corporation, of all entities, in a place that couldn't be farther from the glitz of Disney World.

It's a particularly busy, short-staffed evening, and necessity has forced you to trade your cheap manager's suit for a waiter's apron to serve a large family from northern New Jersey. Hackensack, the same city where your grandmother raised your father before moving to the cleaner air of Cumberland: the tired industrial hub central to the otherwise rural strip-mined stretch of northern Appalachia, where Pennsylvania is separated from West Virginia by a thin strip of Maryland. Where this hotel now stands, offering a convenient stop just off the highway between better destinations. One day, the state of Maryland keeps promising, they'll put a casino in this hotel, creating a reason to stay awhile. But that won't happen for years. For now, the hotel feels like the waypoint it is, infected with a strange sense of impermanence, reflecting the eager-for-elsewhere mindset of its transient guests.

The family's name is Buccelli, and there are eighteen of them crowded into the hotel's private dining room, "PDR" in restaurant-speak, nearly every one of them grossly obese. With a maximum capacity of twenty, you estimate that the PDR is actually over capacity by at least 50 percent based on weight, more so based on sheer noise.

The Buccellis are hell to wait on, constantly shouting over each other in the cramped space, changing seats immediately after ordering and then again between each of four courses, making it nearly impossible to remember who gets what plate. They couldn't care less about the difficulty they're causing. In fact, they make a game of it as the night grinds on and you surprise them by continuing to place their plates correctly, without asking, at each subsequent course. They latch onto your first name, announced by your bougie hotel nametag. So Italian, like theirs. They insert your name into every sentence, repeating it again and again as they try to stymie you at your work.

"Dominic, we all moved again!"

"There's no way Dominic's gonna get it this time."

"No, Dominic's good. Twenty says he gets it right."

"Dominic, honey, can you pass me that wine over there? No, dear, you don't have to pour. I just don't want Tony to drink it all, he gets so loud."

"Jesus, Dominic, you did it again! He did it again! Didn't I tell you? Hand over that twenty, Tony!"

And one of the ladies, wearing a scoop-necked top exposing much of her expansive bosom, currently resting on the table, starts singing the world's worst song, "Dominic-a-nick-a-nick-a-nick-a . . ."

Ohmygawd, you think, already assimilating their familiar accent.

You experience a moment of rare gratitude for your father. Ever since you first met him, when you were fifteen and desperate to escape your stepfather, your father had been intent on forcing his hard-earned restaurant wisdom on you, his often apathetic son. Perhaps making up for all those lost years of fatherhood, perhaps attempting to mitigate an undeniably awkward situation the only way he knew.

Despite the rarity of your gratitude, you were quick to accept the opportunity your father offered less than a year after that first meeting:

to leave your childhood home, your stepfather's home, to move in with your real Dad, to meet your other family, to create a new home. And despite your inclination toward apathy, you quickly learned that creating your new home would require working in your father's restaurant, his true home, where he and your stepmother spent the vast majority of their time. As you learned how to set and bus and finally to wait tables, a skill as worthy of the word "craft" as carpentry, your father insisted, he taught you how to use visual association for just this purpose.

So despite your recent certainty that your days of waiting tables have passed, you find yourself naturally following the Buccelli's movements as they continue to play musical chairs between courses while you deliver tray after tray to the PDR.

Man with Tom Selleck mustache moved from seat three to seat eighteen.

Lady with magnificent cleavage moved from seat eighteen to seat ten.

Too-short red tie moved from seat ten to seat three.

Ungrateful teenager left the room, keep his plate hot until he returns.

You're admittedly frustrated every time you barely manage to slide behind their chairs, pushed out from the table nearly to the walls, accommodating their impressive girths. Plates barely balanced up your arms, you mutter behind them, injecting yourself below the constant roar of their conversation.

"Excuse me, Ms. Buccelli."

"Pardon my reach, Mr. Buccelli."

"Sorry to interrupt, Tony."

"Forgive me, would you mind moving your glass?"

As frustrating as you find serving the Buccellis, you take genuine pleasure in their noise, their New Jersey accents, their unabashed yelling, arguments obviously revisited year after year. They provide a comforting reminder of the better side of your own family. Your Maryland family, the family you weren't allowed to know as a child. The Italian family that originated in Sicily, whose immigrant history and New Jersey accents indicated a class substantially below that of the self-congratulatory WASPs of your stepfather's heritage. The family that helped you escape all the horror your stepfather brought upon you as a child, no matter how ungrateful you were.

"Uncle Frank died in '70, not '69, how many times do I have to tell you?" says Fat Tom Selleck.

"No, no, *no*, you're thinking of Jerry, you idiot. *Jerry* died in '70, Frank died in '69," responds Short Red Tie.

"Who're you calling idiot! Let's ask Ma. She'll know. *Ma!*"

"Yes, dear?" responds the matriarch of the family, Donna Buccelli, the one you marked Steel Blue Hair in your notes and the only person at the table yet to move.

"When did Uncle Frank die, Ma?"

"What, you're asking me? I don't know what I had for breakfast, for crissakes."

"The buffet, Ma! Don't you remember? There were crab legs. For breakfast. Jesus, who could forget that?"

Soon enough, the Buccellis learn that your grandmother is from Sicily via Brooklyn and later Hackensack, that her maiden name is Giarritta, that you still have cousins in northern New Jersey named Romano, and that your own surname is Miller. Despite some confusion resulting from the announcement of your last name, by the time entrees are cleared and dessert menus distributed, you're practically family.

"I couldn't eat another thing," says Fat Tom Selleck.

"Bullshit. Have the molten chocolate cake," says Short Red Tie, recently renamed Contrary Older Brother.

"Ask Dominic. He knows what's good," says Ma Buccelli from her thankfully constant place at seat one.

"Waddaya think, Dominic?" asks Fat Tom Selleck.

"Have the molten chocolate cake," you say, barely restraining yourself from calling him Tom. "It's good for you."

Contrary Older Brother, now at seat eight, erupts into laughter, his shaking belly shaking the table, nearly disrupting the remaining glassware.

"Ohmygawd, Dominic, that's hilarious. It's good for you! I love this guy! Dominic, come over here." You dutifully shimmy to seat eight, smiling as he grabs your arm. "Are you allowed to have some wine?"

You are not allowed to have some wine, but you gladly accept the proffered glass and enjoy a healthy swig, Silver Oak Cabernet, just as bougie and overpriced as the hotel, but delicious nonetheless.

"Here's what I wanna know, Dominic," Contrary Older Brother earnestly says, looking deep into his own glass, tightening his grip on your arm. "I wanna know: How does a *guy*," dramatic drunken pause as he looks up at you, "End up with a *name*," brief interruption as he slurps his wine, "Like Dominic," another pause, "*Miller*. Can you tell me that, please? How is that possible?"

In one of those rare moments when the right words for the right audience in the right circumstance thoughtlessly spill from your tongue, you answer, "When she was like seventeen, Grandma betrayed us to the Irish. From what I understand, Great Grandpa Giarritta was *pissed*."

The Buccellis roar with appreciative laughter. Contrary Older Brother's belly shakes the table again as he shakes your arm, sloshing expensive red wine over your clean, white sleeve.

"Ohmygawd, Dominic, that's rich! Betrayed you to the Irish, did she? I love this guy! Italian and Irish, Jesus H! You're a goddamn barbarian, you!"

Imagine your family, its dynamics, its arguments, all of its factions. Imagine your dinner table. What do you observe? Do the factions gather? Does everyone set aside their petty disagreements, their minor betrayals, at least for a little while? Or do those disagreements get wrestled out at the table for all to see? Who's seated next to each other, comfortable and companionable? Has anyone been placed at opposite ends of the table, safely away from each other? Who's missing from the table altogether? Anyone? If so, do you know why?

Perhaps you know of someone at this table who's been hurt by someone else at this table. It happens all the time, after all. Offender and victim, parent and child, husband and wife, bonded by blood or marriage, all with families, all with a table to visit. Do they acknowledge the truth? Or do they ignore it, silently reassuring themselves that it's for the good of all?

Perhaps you know of such a secret in your family. Perhaps you've heard the unspoken threat, the pressure to stay silent.

What would happen if you refused? What would happen if you exposed the secret? Would your family forgive your betrayal?

Imagine your dinner table.

Are you welcome?

MOTIVE

THE HOLIDAYS HAVE been difficult, as always. Even now, with just a few days remaining in 2010, less than two months until your thirty-third birthday, the week you've spent pretending at normalcy in your childhood home in Litchfield has steadily ratcheted up your anxiety until you find yourself reinhabiting something like your teenage routine of avoidance and silence. By the end of the week, your stepfather has returned to that era as well, exhibiting a frustrated shadow of the rage he constantly directed at you back then. You've sensed a breaking point's approach for days, your sensitivity to your stepfather's mood as highly attuned as ever. The night before your departure, it arrives.

Dinner has been cleared from the table and the kitchen will soon be clean, eliminating your excuse for solitude. You're just finishing the chore routine, the same routine you performed as a boy, decades-old muscle memory making the motions automatic as you tend to the leftovers, load the dishwasher, scrub the pots and pans, wipe down the counters, sweep the floor, and finally bag the trash. Twenty years later, you forget nothing.

Your mother, stepfather, and sisters' voices drift from the living room around the corner, where they recline in front of the fire, some recently recorded piece of your stepfather's music emitting from the speakers at a volume just loud enough to obscure their words. But they clearly sound happy, content. You cannot stifle a snarled *fuck!* as the cheap garbage bag splits beneath its weight, dinner debris spilling out over the freshly cleaned floor.

"Dominic, Jesus, your language," your stepfather's voice comes from behind you, his tone slightly amused but with an edge to it, letting you know that he is not, in fact, amused.

Instead of voicing your oft-considered opinion about his willingness to spend obscene sums on certain things, like archaic musical instruments or vacations in the Hamptons, despite his inclination toward downright miserliness regarding more practical items, like garbage bags or his stepson's education; instead of reminding him that you're nearly thirty-three years old and can use any language you damn well please, especially while cleaning up after the rest of the family as they relax with their full bellies in front of the fire; instead of simply telling him to *fuck off* the way you've always wanted to, you say to your step-father:

"The bag broke."

Your stepfather says, "I can see that, but there's no reason to lose your temper." You retrieve a fresh, thinner-than-paper bag from under the sink and begin trying to pry the damn thing open, your movements abrupt, frustrated, reflecting the anger your words can't. Your step-father continues, "Well don't waste another bag, we can just bring the pail over to the door and dump it all in. Where's the broom? Go out and get the pail, will you?"

And as you always have, you obey your stepfather, forcing the half-opened bag back into its box under the sink, straightening and silently walking for the door. You retrieve the garbage bin from its place on the side of the house, noticing that it's the same one that's been here since you were a boy, a deep circle of ancient Rubbermaid, its bottom split in a wide crescent from years of use beyond reasonable expectation, caus-ing its wheels to swerve in every direction but the one you want. You drag it across the driveway in annoyed jerks, risking spilling yesterday's trash too as you heft it up a step into the breezeway and maneuver it toward the kitchen door, where your stepfather waits with the split bag and half its contents gingerly held before him. He dumps the bag into the pail and turns away, reaching for the broom.

"Bring it closer," he says, and you respond by lifting the barrel up onto the kitchen threshold, watching the split bottom yawn open, one of those cheap garbage bags straining as it bulges out.

"No, don't bring it in," he growls, straightening as he lifts a dust pan overflowing with trash in his left hand, his right barely holding the pile together at arm's length. And so you respond again, stepping back and pulling the garbage bin with you, back into the breezeway just as he turns to tip the dustpan into it. He makes a stumbling motion toward you, his face full of false surprise. "Dammit, Dominic, do you want to make me spill again?"

"Sorry," you say. "Do you want me to get the rest?"

"No, no, I'll do it. Just hold the pail right there."

He finishes sweeping up the rest of the trash as you uselessly hold the pail and look on. He begins breathing heavily, moving in exaggerated jerks, just as you had a few moments ago. He dumps the last of the debris and then holds the broom head over the pail, picking at dust clumps and bits of food stuck in the bristles.

"I guess old habits die hard," he says, with something like a chuckle, not looking at you, continuing to pick at the bristles with angry fingers even after the last of the dust is in the pail.

"What's that?" you ask.

"Don't you remember how often I used to have to tell you to clean the broom after you were done sweeping?"

You remember all too well, the constant criticism often leading to a late-night lecture. *What, is that supposed to be endearing? A fond Christmas memory we share?* you wonder.

"Is that broom as old as this trash bin?" you ask, shocked that you would invite confrontation, fully aware that such a seemingly mild remark would do exactly that. He looks at you sharply, any hint of his earlier feigned amusement dispelled from his face. *Here we go,* you think, oddly relieved. The wait is over, the anxiety of anticipation finally broken. Twenty years later, you can still count on a dirty broom head leading to a lecture.

"Where does all this frustration come from?" he asks, his tone mild even as his face reddens. "Come in here, I want to talk to you." And as you begin dragging the broken trash barrel back outside, he snaps, "Just leave it. We need to talk."

So you leave the broken barrel where it sits and follow him into the kitchen, closing the door behind you. He takes his seat at the kitchen island, resting his elbows on the butcher block counter, propping his chin on folded hands. You reach for your half-empty wine glass on the counter, the only dirty dish remaining in the kitchen.

"We worry about your drinking," he says as you take a sip, assuming your own customary position, leaning against the kitchen sink, opposite him, as far away as you can manage while still facing him. "Think about your father."

"I think about my father all the time," you say, unable to prevent a touch of anger in your voice. "That's why I don't drink vodka." And as soon as you've said it, you recall the Bloody Marys you made for everyone at Christmas brunch a few days earlier. *In honor of Grandpa,* you announced to counter your mother's concern that it was too early for alcohol. Your stepfather and sisters drained the pitcher before you finished cooking the benedicts, leaving you the only person with a drink in hand through the meal.

"Well, we're worried about you," your stepfather continues, standing and rounding the island, striding toward you and the cupboard just behind. He stands closer to you than necessary as he rummages for a glass. "You seem angry. Ever since your divorce." He pauses next to you for a moment, a tall water glass engulfed in his big drummer's hand. He lingers, letting the moment stretch, stoking your discomfort, trying to catch your eye. You purposefully remove your eyes from his hand, avoiding his gaze, looking straight ahead and slightly down, toward the butcher block on the kitchen island, past him, beyond him, resolute for all the wrong reasons.

He finally moves away, opening the refrigerator and retrieving an open bottle of white wine. He pours the remaining contents into his glass, filling it more than halfway. He reclaims his seat at the kitchen island and sits quietly for a moment, turning the glass in slow circles between those thick, calloused fingers. Finally, he takes a long swig, returns his glass to the butcher block, leans forward on his elbows, and so intently says, "Your mother and I are concerned that you've become quite a bitter man. Why do you think that is?"

Instead of responding that his phrasing indicates his fundamental lack of understanding; instead of pointing out that he might be bitter too, if he'd recently lost everything in a difficult divorce; instead of reminding him that you're nearly thirty-three years old and have yet to earn a bachelor's degree, and the best work you can aspire to is waiting tables in a half-decent restaurant; instead of spitting at him, *how could you, of all the people in the world, ask me that question*, you say to your stepfather:

"I don't know."

Because twenty years later, you forget nothing.

LINEAGE

YOUR GRANDMOTHER'S NAME was Josephine, and she may not have been seventeen, but she *was* quite young, no more than twenty, when she married the Irishman. And this act of defiance really was considered a betrayal by the rest of her family. It wasn't her youth, of course. It was her unacceptable rebellion, her taking her life's most pivotal decision from its rightful makers: her father and uncles, even her older brother.

Sicilian immigrant families with children born during the Depression shared simple expectations. Young men were to seek gainful employment, legal or otherwise, as soon as they were physically able. In rare cases, higher education might be considered, but only if three prerequisites were met, in descending order of priority:

1. The young man's studies created no additional financial burden for the family;
2. the young man was relatively light skinned, and;
3. the young man was exceptionally talented intellectually or creatively or showed particular aptitude for a skilled trade.

The young Sicilian woman, however, was expected to eschew the idea of gainful employment, to never even consider college, and to dutifully keep house while supporting the work and egos of her male betters. This arrangement would continue until a suitable Sicilian suitor eventually took her into his own home, where she would be expected to dutifully keep house for her husband while supporting his work and ego. And, of course, immediately get to work perpetuating the cycle by bearing children and raising them in accordance with the long-established Law of Sicilian Men.

Josephine flatly refused to obey the law. Her older brother was one of those lucky few deemed fit for college, attending first the Naval Academy in Annapolis, followed by medical school on the GI Bill. Grandma's sister followed the law to the letter, marrying a respectable, Cadillac-driving Sicilian with the surname Romano and producing children at regular intervals, four in total.

Josephine simply didn't believe that her brother was any smarter than she was. In fact, quite the opposite. And her complexion was perfectly fair, while her brother's was really quite olive. Her father's refusal to allow her to consider a job, let alone college, festered throughout her teenage years, as her brother traveled the world and became a pathologist. With both her siblings out of the house, Josephine found herself unwilling to wait for the right Sicilian man.

Your grandmother's purpose was simple, that universal motive shared by young people of all backgrounds: Freedom. Independence. Escape.

His name was Joseph Miller. If his Irish heritage were ignored, he was undoubtedly a catch. The man who would become your grandfather was in his thirties, handsome, and well established in a career that earned him a decent living. He drove a Jaguar. More important, he owned his own home, a tidy Victorian row house in one of the nicer areas of Bergen County. The Law of Sicilian Men clearly confirmed that no matter how much the family disapproved of the match, this house would now be hers.

"Besides," Grandma often reminded you, "my kids are as white as they come. They sure as hell got to go to college. And he was still a Catholic, for crissakes."

You could never know when Grandma figured out that she'd simply traded one misogynistic house for another. In her case, it seems clear that her new home with her somewhat foreign husband proved worse than the Sicilian counterpart she had gone to so much trouble to escape.

Grandma gave birth to your father about two years after marrying Joe. When your father was a child, your grandfather's habit was to spend his evenings at a pub across the street from his office at Westinghouse, drinking Scotch and paying three dollars for blow jobs in his parked Jaguar. When your grandfather finally came home, he often beat your father, his half-breed Sicilian son, as he slept in his bed, waking him up with his fists and wailing away until the small boy's cries subsided into unconsciousness.

Your grandmother stayed married to Joe for another fifteen years. She finally divorced him in 1969. Grandma never confirmed that she also experienced physical abuse at her ex-husband's hands, but her brother, the pathologist, eventually told you as much.

You met your grandfather in 1994, when you escaped your own abusive home. He was physically deteriorated, made ancient by arthritis, his neck permanently skewed toward his left shoulder. He appeared totally incapable of hurting anyone. He lived with your father and your new stepmother, and while years would pass before you learned the darker details of the family history, you instantly despised him.

Something about him reminded you of your stepfather.

CIVIL ACTION

YOUR DECISION TO tell arrives on the afternoon of Tuesday, January 11, 2011, little more than a week after your stepfather expressed concern about your "bitterness." In six weeks, you will turn thirty-three. The decision has likely been coming for years, for more than a decade, really, perhaps ever since you first escaped your stepfather's home, sixteen years ago. Perhaps even earlier.

But on this cold, sunny January afternoon, sitting at your desk in your study in your new home in Vermont, where you've recently relocated in what feels like another escape, this time from your second home with your second family, your Maryland family, later your home with your wife, now your ex-wife, the decision seems to arrive all at once. As you sit at your desk, chronicling the events of recent weeks in your journal, an exercise in reflection mercilessly leading you back in time, to your darkest memories, you abruptly find yourself out of excuses for procrastination. And it suddenly seems clear that all your years of silence have been just that. Procrastination. A flaw akin to leaving the chores unfinished. The inexcusable failing your stepfather raged against in your childhood, come full-circle.

Intellectually, you're aware that your silence represents something well beyond the idea of procrastination, something unfathomably deeper. To break that silence would require much more than the opposite of laziness. It would require something beyond energy, beyond courage, an unnameable strength. And yet, in this moment, it seems clear that you can't wait another moment. You must seek that unnameable strength, the opposite of a lifetime of silence. Unsettled, angry, and above all, terrified, you wonder, *why now?*

Perhaps it's the relationship you've recently entangled yourself in, an affair with a married woman, with two young sons and an abusive husband. Perhaps it's all the hours you've spent in conversation with her, offering support and trying to help her navigate her presumed exit from a home in which she'd been constantly belittled and viciously beaten, bloodied, dragged by her hair, countless horror stories through which you selfishly assure her that there is life beyond divorce.

Recently she'd observed her husband's rage directed beyond her, apparently a less ignorable catalyst than her own years of suffering. Escalating, you're certain, her husband had turned on her cousin, a dear friend, and even their son, the elder of her children. He'd beaten the boy, not yet ten years old, with a shoe, publicly, in the halls of a hotel in which you yourself have worked, allowing you to visualize the scene with sickening accuracy.

Because you love her, because you trust her, because she is the mother of young boys, and because you so quickly, naively assume that your relationship will grow beyond her inevitable divorce, you feel the need to share something of your story with her. You tell her about your stepfather. You tell her more than you've ever told anyone.

And even as she considers the concept of shared custody, weighing the specter of an abusive father's presence against the unknown toll of a father largely absent, even as she continues to vacillate over whether she'll leave her husband at all, her response to your confession is to ask, *Why haven't you done anything about it? Why haven't you exposed him? What if your stepfather is hurting other children as we speak?*

But perhaps your need to tell started earlier. Perhaps it was your own divorce, the ugly end of the seven-year marriage that consumed most of your twenties. The marriage that you never wanted but allowed to happen with no resistance, your twenty-two-year-old self still essentially that broken teenage boy, unable to take a stand and say *wait a minute, I'm not sure I want this,* let alone the vehement *no* that would later become clear as the only true response.

Instead, you allowed the years to pile up and slip away, year after year, everything done right. The right jobs, the right house, the right cars, the right mutual funds, assuring yourself that all this was the result of the right marriage even as each of those years became a wasted haze in your memory almost as soon as it passed. Every moment of each of those years a lie, a lie growing ever larger, interest on principal compounding every day, spreading false tendrils into every facet of your life and beyond. The biggest lie you'd ever told.

What could possibly expose such a lie? Such a huge lie, a lie with years of foundation, a lie perfectly reinforced, believed by everyone around you. A lie that you yourself couldn't afford not to believe.

The answer presented itself when your wife informed you of her pregnancy. You were going to be a father.

Weeks passed, as surreal as all the years that came before. Her belly grew, and you maintained the lie, everything done right. The right birthing center, the right nursery colors, the right crib, the right car seat. But even as you fed the lie, you found yourself observing it from a slightly removed point of view, considering, detached, rediscovering that old, familiar sense of dissociation even as you came closer to the truth.

And as you watched, the foundation began to crumble, the walls of your carefully constructed lie settling, cracking at the seams. By the time the baby arrived, your child, your son, the walls had fallen, the weak, false foundation fully exposed. And in the rubble, the only thing that survived was that long lost *no* you'd tried to bury under the right house.

Or perhaps you're just sick of lying. Perhaps you're sick of *his* lies. Perhaps you simply can't stand another moment of your family's considering you broken, *bitter*, without knowing why.

Bitter? You'll show them *bitter*.

"I'm so sorry, Dominic," your sister says, wiping her eyes and trying to compose herself.

You've decided to start with Christina, the elder of your half sisters, now twenty-six years old, pursuing a career in early childhood education in Burlington. Both of your sisters have settled in Vermont, one of the reasons you decided to make it your own home. *Because family is important*, you told yourself, despite the underlying, perhaps truer thought, *family is complicated. Family hurts.*

105

But if there exists any way to mitigate the complications and pain of family, surely your sisters, your peers in experience, at least to some degree, represented the best chance. So you rented a house within a couple miles of Christina's apartment, and the two of you have become quite close since your move. And as the older of your two sisters, she represents the safest place to begin. Perhaps she will be of some help in telling Sarah, the youngest.

Tina agrees to join you for dinner that night, thrilled at being invited out for a "date night" alone with her brother. Guilt floods through you when you receive her texted response, a string of exclamation points and smiley faces in dots and dashes. But how can you possibly prepare her?

You pick her up at her apartment shortly after six o'clock and drive to her favorite Thai restaurant, Tiny Thai, a bustling little place that always brings to mind your sister's most widely used moniker, Tiny Tina. She'd been tiny at every stage of her life, and still is as an adult, nothing in her petite frame indicating any relation to you, her face reflecting your grandmother's more than anyone else's, your stepfather's mother, the Tough Cookie. Tina could be a Tough Cookie in her own right, but tonight there's no toughness in her.

You'd given no hint of what you wanted to discuss when you arranged the date, of course, but she picks up on your mood after just a few moments in the restaurant. You manage some small talk on the ride over, appropriately exclaiming in all the right places as she regales you with inappropriate work stories, which kids are chronic masturbators, which "extra-Vermonty" mothers continue breastfeeding their children well into toddlerhood. How you wish these could be the most inappropriate behaviors discussed tonight.

But by the time you're seated, at a table separated from the next by barely a foot, you've run out of small talk. You thought Tiny Thai would be a good idea, not just because it was Tina's favorite but because it was always so busy. Nearby diners and a server's constant interruptions might prevent the tension from becoming unbearable.

Now you aren't so sure. What if your neighbors overhear? What if you burst out crying, as you feel you might at any moment? What if Tina does the same?

Her silence projects her concern as you toy with your plate of fiery drunken noodles and drink more than your share of the bottle of sauvignon blanc. Only then are you able to begin.

She can't meet your eyes as you tell her about some of the things her father did to you. You'd hoped to avoid tears, but before long the two of you are crying quietly together, hesitantly in the crowded restaurant, you as you tell, your sister as she absorbs, your heads leaning toward each other across the narrow table. You take her hand and will her to say something.

And when she finally speaks, her few words overwhelm you. "I'm so sorry, Dominic," she says, and you immediately request the check.

Out of the restaurant, in your car, your emotions are finally allowed out unchecked. But still you hesitate, unable to get beyond quiet crying. The drive to her apartment takes five minutes, and you're unable to speak. You double-park in front of her building's entrance, and then you sit quietly together for a few moments more. The temperature is in the single digits and falling, your Subaru's heater blasting hot air at your face, quickly chapping your tears into dried salt, irritating your eyes.

Your sister finally breaks the silence, asking, "Did he rape you?"

Such a concise question. As soon as you hear it, you realize that you've been waiting for it. Something like it, anyway, some indication of that perfectly human need for specificity. And it isn't until that moment that you acknowledge, "I'm not sure. I think he might have."

That answer obviously requires further explanation, but in that moment you have none. Your memories of rape—*real* rape, as defined on television by *Law and Order Special Victims Unit*—penetration, the ultimately forbidden act your sister obviously means, feel chopped up, haunting glimpses that often lack details of time and place but regularly invade your darkest dreams. While you're sure that your stepfather had, in fact, raped you, you don't want to say anything that you can't be absolutely certain of. And you don't want to hurt your sister any more than you already have.

You tell her, "I know that there was oral sex. I know it happened often, countless times. I don't know if he raped me, not for sure, but I think, maybe, he did."

Tina lets out a terrible, gut-wrenching sob. It lasts only a moment. She sighs heavily, nodding, and exits the car.

She leans back inside long enough to say, "I love you," and abruptly turns away, swinging the door shut, walking deliberately toward her apartment building, and quickly disappearing inside.

After you lose sight of her, your own emotions finally spill over. You can't stop crying, really crying, sobbing over the steering wheel as you drive home. You hate hurting your sister, you *hate* sharing this knowledge. It's the first time you remember crying like that as an adult.

But that seems fitting, you realize, as human as your sister's need to know exactly what happened. As hard as this is, as much as you hate it, perhaps you're on the right track.

The following day, Wednesday, January 12, after a fitful sleep filled with nightmares of rape, you tell your youngest sister, Sarah. Officially, Sarah is your roommate. But she's rarely home, preferring to spend most nights with her boyfriend, who lives about an hour away. Sarah had spent the last few days with him and returned home late in the evening. Despite having broached the subject just the night before, you find yourself full of new trepidation as you anticipate telling her. This time, you figure it best to have the conversation in private, at home.

When she arrives, you force yourself to start in immediately, declaring a reprieve of the indoor smoking ban. The two of you sit facing each other at your kitchen table, drinking cheap red wine and smoking American Spirits one after the other. She's a nonsmoker but smokes almost as much as you that night.

You've always shared a special relationship with your youngest sister. Ten years your junior, she was only six when you left home. On the rare occasions you returned to Litchfield for visits, she often called you "Daddy Dominic," identifying you somewhere on a spectrum between older brother and favorite uncle. Now that she's twenty-two, the two of you have enjoyed getting to know each other as adults during this first time you've lived together since her early childhood.

She helps you by softly asking leading questions and rubbing your knee, encouraging you to say as much as you feel the need to say. She never asks for specifics about the abuse you experienced at her father's hands, never asks about rape, and never once drops her gaze. That helps too.

There are more tears, of course, shed more freely in the privacy of your home. She holds you and mutters *I love you* and *I'm so sorry* and *I'm glad you finally told me.*

Those last words shock you, *I'm glad you finally told me.* You can't quite believe her words, but you're deeply grateful to her for saying them. She *wants* to know, or at least, she wants you to believe that she wants to know. You find yourself pleasantly infected by the kindness that indicates, her thoughtful aim. Here is your youngest sister, too young to have any memory of what the day-to-day of your childhood actually looked like, gently manipulating you in an apparently selfless effort to make you feel better. To try to make your confession okay for you. When you finally fall into bed, thoroughly exhausted and emotionally spent, you sleep better than the night before.

On Thursday, you make an error. You'd intended to drive to Connecticut at the end of the week to speak to your mother and stepfather in person, but it occurred to you that you couldn't be sure to get them both in the same place at the same time. You need your mother there, of course, but you feel that it's of paramount importance that you speak to your stepfather alone first. Ultimately, you want your mother to hear it directly from him.

You call your mother at work to ask what their weekend schedule is like. You tell her that you're driving down and need to talk to them both, but you want to talk to her husband first. Will he be home?

Your mother instantly falls apart. Why do you need to talk to your stepfather first? Why can't you just tell her what's going on?

And the worst: "Dominic, what the fuck? You're scaring me."

You're certain that you've never heard your mother swear like that before, not in seriousness, certainly not directed at you. You don't attempt to make any excuses, just tell her that you'll explain the next day.

But when you hang up, you realize that you can't allow her to worry that long. So you email your stepfather, telling him what you've done and what you intend to do. He should call you.

He does so almost immediately. This time, at least, there is more shouting than tears.

"How dare you tell my girls?" he thunders. "Who do you think you are?"

Instead of apologizing or remaining silent, your first, most powerful inclinations, inclinations reinforced by nearly every year you've lived, you remind him that *his* girls are also *your* sisters, that you have a relationship with each of them separate from his claim as their father. Talking past his increasing fury, you remind him that, ostensibly, by his own oft-repeated claim, you are his son. No matter that you don't want to be his son, that you never wanted to be his son, if he claims you as much his child as his daughters, why should you have less right to them than him?

"So who do you think *you* are? Who are you to tell me I can't talk to my sisters?" you finally finish.

That isn't the end of it, of course. In an eerie return to the dynamic of your childhood, the two of you speak in circles for hours. It's so hard not to fall back into your old, established pattern, so difficult not to succumb to exhaustion, to just let him have it, to tell him that you're sorry, to allow him to *win*, to do as he will, to protect his lies.

But you don't do any of that. You resist that lazily seductive urge, somehow managing to maintain your resolve. And at the end, finally, it's your stepfather retreating, crying, succumbing to your will. You've finally found at least some of that unnameable strength, the opposite of a lifetime of silence, finally managed to access your anger, finally found the proper outlet for Gozer, that frighteningly strong, self-righteous part of yourself, the subversive keeper of all your rage.

Freed to speak as he will, Gozer demands that your stepfather tell his wife what he'd done to you as a child. Immediately. And then he should tell his daughters as well. There is no manipulation, no capitulation, nothing indirect in your demands. Gozer simply tells your stepfather what he has to do.

And amazingly, finally, your stepfather does as told.

And then comes the phone call from your mother, with neither shouts nor tears, just a terrible tone of defeated exhaustion.

"Why, Dominic?" she asks. "Why are you doing this?"

COFFEE TALK

- *Kwauffeee*—Coffee, a drink made exclusively from canned Medaglia d'Oro preground espresso in a percolator, best drunk black or with a single packet of artificial sweetener. To be enjoyed all day, every day, each cup complete with saucer and accompanied by at least one cigarette—Mores, the long, skinny brown things in the narrow red and brown package. They smell like burning shit.
- *Twaulk*—Talk, or more specifically, gossip, an activity that should always be accompanied by a number of cups of *kwauffeee*. And the obligatory cigarettes. Josephine's primary form of recreation.

Your grandmother represents the only authority in your seventeen years of life that you at least attempt to respect. You test your boundaries with her as you do with everyone, of course, but never to any extreme. You love her and, in fact, just plain like her too much to risk really hurting her. Perhaps it's her natural inclination to be contrary, a quality you've often wished for in your own mother, discovered for the first time in the mother of your father. Perhaps this woman would have saved you, if only she'd been present.

Despite your pure intentions toward your grandmother, you occasionally push her a bit too far, instances Grandma refers to as "shenanigans." Often your shenanigans involve *smoking the pot*, extra emphasis on *the*. You've spent your junior year in Maryland enjoying your newfound freedom from your stepfather and traveling from one bag of pot to another, usually finding them within the halls of your Catholic school. Your father and stepmother are endlessly busy with their restaurants, and during that first year in Cumberland, you often stay at Grandma's house so that some semblance of parental supervision can be maintained over you.

The first time your shenanigans stretch well beyond Grandma's limit, you've been at a party in Frostburg, the college town about fifteen minutes up the highway. You drive home around two in the morning, well after your midnight curfew. Any reasonable person might expect a woman in her seventies to be fast asleep at that hour.

Not Grandma. Her waking schedule generally runs from about noon until anywhere between two and four in the morning with *Fox News* offering a constant soundtrack played at a level entirely too loud, although often ignored even by her. She lives in a small house with two upstairs bedrooms, one of which is reserved for your use. The other is entirely devoted to her wardrobe. You believe there's a bed somewhere in that room, but you can't be sure. Grandma sleeps on the living room sofa, making it impossible to avoid her no matter the hour.

She's heard you parking her car, and when you walk in you find her standing in the kitchen, wearing an opulent, shockingly pink, furry robe you've never seen before. There are rarely repeats in Grandma's wardrobe, including her nightwear.

She's about to make kwauffeee, a sure sign of an impending twaulk. You may have preemptively redeemed yourself a bit by remembering to pick up the can of Medaglia d'Oro she instructed you to buy on your way home. She'd run out of it during the day and had to resort to a lesser brand, not a healthy situation for her mood, and through her angry look you see just a hint of a smile as you wordlessly open the can and reach past her to scoop a ridiculous amount of the stuff into the coffee maker.

"Where were you, *Dominic*," she demands.

"Frostburg," you answer, turning on the percolator. She's behind you now. You can practically feel her fury baking off her. Or maybe it's some strange sort of energy radiating from her ridiculous robe. You're quite high, and the thought of her robe radiating an energy field puts you in danger of hysterics. You bite your lip hard and put off turning to face her by carefully wiping up some spilled grounds and returning them to the can. Coffee is not wasted in this house.

"Frostburg," she repeats, and you realize your mistake. "*Dominic.* With MY car?" She grabs your arm and spins you around.

Your grandmother stands perhaps just slightly over five feet tall. At seventeen, you're partial to thick-soled Doc Martens. You tower over her. Does that give her pause?

Absolutely not. She slaps you across the face. Not a slap meant to hurt, necessarily, simply to shame. You apparently have too much of her in you, however. These days, you have no shame. The slap cuts through your pot-addled thoughts and makes you angry.

"I didn't drink," you lie.

"Bullshit!" she says. "Just like your father."

"Don't bullshit a bullshitter, right?" you sneer, anticipating the next line in this established routine.

She tries to slap you again, but you catch her wrist before she can land it. Usually this absolutely infuriates her—how dare you interfere when she's of a mind to hit you?

So you're surprised, even a little concerned, when this time it seems to deflate her instead. You feel her arm go slack and let her wrist go.

"Make the kwauffeee," she tells you, heading off to the living room.

Mystified, but admittedly relieved, you do so. Cream and a cube of raw sugar for you ("Such a snob, Dominic, I should never have let your mother take you away to Connecticut"), black for her in those days. You'll remember the small cups and their saucers so clearly—some innocuous Bon-Ton department store design, pink to match her electric robe.

"Bring me my cigarettes!" you hear from the living room over the drone of *Fox News*, which hasn't decreased in volume a bit. You cast around for one of the dozen or so open packs littering the house, musing that there's probably a pack or three on the coffee table under the constant pile of newspaper debris right in front of her, but sure enough you find one in the junk bowl on the kitchen counter. You carefully set her coffee and pack of Mores on top of the newspapers on the table, resisting the urge to gather everything up and put it somewhere—anywhere—else. She looks at you expectantly, waiting.

You're sure that your grandmother has lit a few of her own cigarettes in her life. She must have—you can't imagine her ever not smoking just because there isn't a man around to light her cigarette. That said, you feel sure that these instances have been relatively rare. Your hesitation to actually retrieve a cigarette from the pack, hand it to her and then light it damns you further. Too late, you do so now. She inhales in a way and to a degree you've never been able to match, or even understand, eventually blowing a noxious cloud out in your direction with a loud exhale.

Waving away the smog, you go to the television and turn down the volume to a barely audible whisper. To turn it all the way down, or, gawd forbid, turn the awful thing off, would only further damn you. Even turning the volume down can be dangerous, but you simply can't bear the angry drone of *Fox News*.

For once, she doesn't complain about the lack of volume, and you know this is going to be a serious twaulk, beyond her typical gossip. You take your usual chair, the only one in the room that doesn't face the television and the angry white men on it.

"Have you been smoking the pot?" she asks in all seriousness, and you're done. You burst out laughing.

"What's so funny?" she asks, her tone surprisingly mild. "I'm serious here."

You try to control yourself, fishing out your pack of Parliaments, lighting one and reaching for your coffee. You love your grandmother for never criticizing your own smoking habit, which pales in comparison to hers.

"The pot, Grandma," you say, unable to prevent her accent from creeping into your voice. "Yes. I've been smoking the pot." Your laughter subsides a bit. The cigarette helps.

"Don't you get smart with me, *honey*," she begins. *Honey.* That's better than the ultimately serious address—*Young Man*. You may be safe for the moment, but you're feeling the laughter bubbling up in you again. You already know the next line.

"I'll slap you right in your puss," she says.

To be slapped in one's puss is not, in fact, the filthy sexual act that you imagined the first time you heard her utter the phrase. You can't be sure exactly what you imagined, really, if anything, it's just that the word, puss, seems so . . . dirty.

It's actually pretty innocuous. What this second generation Sicilian woman is saying to you in her mysterious language is that she's going to smack you in the mouth. Still, even knowing this, it never fails to reduce you to hilarity whenever she yells "puss" at you in any context, especially when there's an audience. Which is often the case. No shame, your Grandma.

"You can't drive when you've been smoking the pot, Dominic," she continues.

"Grandma, it's not like drinking," you say.

"Oh, I have no doubt there was some of that going on too, up there in Frostburg with all those college boys. You can't bullshit a bullshitter, Dominic." You resist the urge to mouth the phrase as she says it.

"Grandma, I had a beer or two," you say, which is remarkably close to the truth.

"Whatever, you're seventeen years old, you shouldn't be drinking with those older boys, and you certainly shouldn't be driving home in the middle of the night after doing drugs."

"They were girls, Grandma," you say. The point here is to distract her, and this topic is generally a sure bet.

"Oh, knowing you, I'm sure they were! And when do I get to meet any of these girls? These *older* girls?"

"They're just friends, Grandma." She takes another epic drag on her cigarette, blowing out a dirty cumulous cloud between you.

"Well, you seem to have quite a few 'friends,' Dominic. And do they all do drugs like you? Do they all smoke the pot?" She's unusually focused tonight. Damn.

"Everybody smokes a little pot, Grandma. It's no big deal."

"Don't give me that line of bull, *Dominic*." How many times can she use your name in the course of a conversation? Every syllable venomously succinct—Dom-in-ic. Spitting mad.

"Grandma, it's really not much different than this," you say, gesturing with your cigarette.

"Don't try that line on me, honey," she says, and you're relieved not to hear your name spit at you again. "Your Uncle Glenny used to try the same thing. And you know what I did? Well, one day I figured I'd find out for myself."

You wonder whether you've heard correctly.

"What do you mean, Grandma?" you ask. "You tried the pot?"

"You bet I did!" she says. "I wasn't going to let that scoundrel pull the wool over my eyes."

"When was that?" you ask, leaning forward.

"I don't know, Dominic, your uncle was still in high school. Probably about your age. He used to come home high as a kite all the time. He was into the musical group, the Grateful Deads, do you know them? Horrible. He'd even smoke his pot cigarettes in the house! Right there in his room, listening to that racket. As if I wouldn't know he wasn't just smoking cigarettes. That stuff smells *awful*," she says.

"Anyways, I would argue and argue with him, but I was a single mother, you know. In the seventies, *Dominic*. Things were different then. Your grandfather wasn't around, thank gawd. But I could've used him to knock some sense into that boy, that's for sure.

"In any case, I got sick of not knowing what he was twaulking about. I had a friend at work, Angela, a nice young Italian girl, but she smoked the pot. She was always trying to get me to go out back and smoke pot cigarettes with her. I always refused, of course. At work? Are you crazy? But one day I told her I'd like to try some—but only after work, Dominic, okay? I would never do drugs on the job."

"It's not drugs, Grandma." You can't help it.

"Shut up. It is, just like the cocaine or anything else I hear about on the TV," pointing at *Fox News* with her long, ugly cigarette. "Anyways, after work one day, I met Angela by the dumpster, and she hands me this crooked little cigarette. So I smoked it."

You imagine your grandmother taking one of her epic drags, likely even more epic back then, when she had young lungs, before she survived the breast cancer. You can't decide whether to shudder or smile.

"Are you listening to me? So anyways, I smoke the thing. Really, I thought it tasted pretty good. But I tell you what, *Dominic*, when I sat in my car I couldn't decide where to put my key. Do you hear me? I couldn't figure out how to put my car key in the ignition! And you try to tell me you can drive on the pot!"

You try to interject, but she's at peak now.

"And do you have any idea how hard it is to drive on the New Jersey Turnpike? Even sober? Well, try it stoned. Terrified, Dominic. I—was— terrified. And the whole time, you know the only thing I could think of?" Looking at you, actually expecting a response now.

"What, Grandma?" you ask.

"Blimpie," she says.

"Blimpie?"

"You know, Dominic, Blimpie, the sandwich shop? All I could think of the whole time was getting my hands on the biggest Blimpie I could. And that's exactly what I did. I don't even remember ordering the thing. All I remember is sitting in my car in the parking lot because I was too embarrassed to be around the people in the store, eating my Blimpie. One of the big ones, *Dominic*. A foot long. Can you imagine? Me? I ate that whole thing. Ruined my outfit, too, I got mayonnaise all over my-self. And when I finally got home, your Uncle Glenny was standing in the door. He was worried about me, imagine that! I came in the door, and do you know what he said? Do you?"

"What, Grandma?"

"He said, *Ma!* Are you stoned? And do you know what, Dominic? That kid of mine was *horrified*. Horrified! Just think! His own mother! Stoned! I couldn't help myself! I burst out laughing!"

"I know how that goes," you say.

"Oh, I'll just bet you do. Anyways, the next day I told him—don't you ever—ever!—try to tell me you can drive on the pot. Because you can't. I know. And do you know what? Do you know what, *Dominic*?"

"What, Grandma?"

"Well, I don't know that he *never* smoked the pot again." You smile inwardly, knowing full well that Uncle Glenn, highly successful corpo-rate accounting guru that he's become, spent his college years following his beloved Grateful Deads and smoking as much of the pot as possible along the way — the CEO stoner, you've taken to calling him. "But your Uncle Glenny never came home stoned — ever — again. Not that I ever saw, anyways. And look at how successful he is! You do want to be successful, don't you, Dominic?"

Even at that age, you're not at all sure that you want the success she's describing, but you dutifully nod your head. Grandma deserves that much respect, at least.

"Well," she says, "There you go. If you want to be successful, just stop smoking the pot. And don't you ever let me find you driving my car stoned again, *young man*."

DEPOSITION

THE DAY AFTER you told Sarah—Friday, January 14, 2011—the day immediately established in your memory as the longest day you've yet lived, you drive from your home in Burlington to Litchfield. Typically about a five-hour trip, it's nearly doubled by an unexpected blizzard. You arrive much later than you'd intended, around ten o'clock. Perhaps that's for the best.

When she greets you at the door, your mother doesn't offer a hug. Perhaps you should feel surprised by how little her lack of touch affects you, but in fact, you aren't surprised. For this visit, perhaps for the first time in your childhood home, you're all business. It feels right.

Your stepfather hovers behind your mother with an expression you've never seen on his face and have trouble immediately identifying. You decide that it's supposed to be contrite. You see only manipulation.

"I think I burned dinner, but it's on the stove if you want any," your mother says in that same tired, defeated voice you heard on the phone the night before. You haven't experienced that tone from her since your childhood. It was a long drive in bad conditions, but you feel neither tired nor hungry.

"No, thanks," you say.

"Why don't we talk in the living room?" your stepfather asks. Shamefully aware of how easily he can force you to his will, you hate to let him exert even the slightest control. But you're unable to deny the sensibleness of his suggestion.

You follow him into the living room, a sprawling area with lots of seats, a fireplace, and no television. He seats himself at one end as you take the opposite, viscerally reminded that this has always been your natural seating arrangement: you, as far away from him as possible. Your mother sits on the couch in between.

"We've been talking all day," your stepfather begins, his tone so reasonable.

You cut him off.

"I'd like to hear what Mom has to say," you say.

Your mother takes a few moments to begin. You wait silently.

Finally, she says, "Well, Dominic, I just don't know."

I don't know. You don't know what you'd hoped for, but *I don't know* certainly wasn't it.

After another long pause, she continues. She expresses her concern that this revelation could destroy the family. Furthermore, it could destroy their livelihood. She speaks about a life separate from your stepfather. She talks about everything you've thought of during the years you kept your secret. In all of her words, you hear the prompting of your stepfather.

Finally, you allow him to speak.

"I'm willing to do whatever it takes," he says, his tone expressing willingness totally out of character. It seems like the right answer. It's positive, forward thinking, divorced from his usual self-righteous vocabulary. You give him your ultimatum.

"I need to be assured that there haven't been others," you say. He rushes to assure you just that, but you cut him off. "I don't believe you. I can't. I can't believe that I'm the only one."

There's a lot of discussion that night, surprisingly subdued words that immediately turn surreal, slipping from your mind. You'd been prepared for anger, prepared to respond with your own, to unleash Gozer in all his glorious rage.

You only come close once, at the end, when your stepfather begins ruminating about suicide, wondering aloud how he can possibly continue living after this revelation. At that, Gozer finally peeks through, infusing your words with fury and bringing an abrupt close to the conversation.

"Shut the fuck up," you say. "You fucking coward. I survived you; you can sure as hell survive me." And once again, your stepfather responds promptly to your anger, to Gozer. He shuts right up.

After that there doesn't seem to be anything else to say. You stand and make your way back to the kitchen, your mother and stepfather slowly following. You pour yourself a glass of water to take to bed, aware of them watching you.

You say your goodnights. There is no touching. Just "goodnight" as you fill your water glass. Your mother and stepfather retreat upstairs to their separate bedrooms. You cross the breezeway into your mother's studio, once your grandmother's in-law suite, where you'll try to get a few hours of sleep on the pullout bed before leaving early in the morning. Before your stepfather wakes up.

You're wearing nothing but your jeans when your stepfather abruptly comes through the door. He reaches out to hug you.

In that instant, for the first time in your life, you are finally able to act on the fact that you absolutely cannot bear his touch. You shove him away, hard.

He says, "I just wanted to tell you I'm sorry."

You say, "Thank you"—and, that simply, he leaves. You want to bask in the satisfaction of causing him awkwardness for once. So why is there none?

You're in bed when your mother comes to you. She's waited until your stepfather was fully asleep, just as you used to wait for him before sneaking out at night. She quietly closes the door and sits down on the bed, softly calling your name.

"Dominic?" she asks.

You raise yourself up on your elbows, already perfectly alert.

"I'm so sorry, baby," she says, and finally you hear what you've really needed to hear from her. You take your mother in your arms as she crumbles into sobbing.

"I didn't know. I always knew he was too hard on you, but I really had no idea that he was doing that," she says.

In that moment, you believe her. *Need* to believe her. You have your answer. Your mother hadn't known. She really hadn't known.

You hold your mother for a little while, long enough to assure her that you believe her. Finally, she stands.

"I love you, baby," she says, and kisses you on the cheek. "I love you so much."

"I love you too, Mom," you reassure her, already doubting her.

After she leaves, sleep seems impossible. But eventually, you drift. And you dream of the boy you were.

. . . .

The whole family is walking at Topsmead, a beautiful nature preserve a few miles from home. Grandma and Grandpa are there, as well as the boy's uncle and his uncle's new wife. The boy's mother is nervous about leaving the roasting turkey unattended. It's Thanksgiving.

The family walks the grounds for an hour or so, until the boy's mother says she needs to return home to check the turkey. The boy's uncle is right in the middle of the characteristic Marshall mania, however, very like Stepfather's. There's just enough snow on the ground, and he's begun building forts for a grand snowball fight in one of the meadows. The boy's mother has been uncharacteristically participating, having fun and pitching in with the fort building. Stepfather volunteers to go home and check the turkey. He asks the boy to come with him.

"Leave the snowball fight to the girls," he says. "You always win, anyway."

The boy sees no way to refuse without raising questions. He is forced to agree.

The boy joins Stepfather in the car. Stepfather is silent as he pulls out of the parking lot. They'd argued the night before. Chores, likely, and the boy's failure to complete them properly.

Stepfather stops at Mobil first, for cigarettes, then drives straight home. He instructs the boy to wait for him in the living room while he checks the turkey.

Stepfather joins the boy in the living room a few moments later, carrying a glass of whiskey. Jack Daniels, of course, its sour aroma assaulting the boy's nose. The boy sits on the edge of the couch, but Stepfather sits directly next to him, his thighs pressed close against the boy's. The November afternoon is near its end, but the sun is still up. The room is bordered by bare windows on every side but one.

Stepfather speaks kindly to the boy, but the boy doesn't hear his words. As Stepfather speaks, he undoes the boy's pants. He touches the boy's penis, gets it hard. He takes the boy in his mouth for a bit but does not finish. Stepfather stands and undoes his own pants. He forcibly leans the boy over the armrest of the couch, pushing the boy's pants down, his shirt up, exposing his ass, all while speaking kindly.

He rapes the boy on that couch, in the daylight, with the windows unobstructed, on a holiday, when the rest of the family might show up at any moment. He rapes the boy on that couch, holding him down, face down, the boy's head mashed into the armrest. As Stepfather thrusts, the boy's head slides forward until his neck is wedged against the armrest. Stepfather holds the boy's hands behind his back with one hand and grips the boy by the back of the neck with the other. As Stepfather continues, he forces the boy's neck down onto the armrest harder and harder.

The boy has no knowledge of the fact that asphyxiation heightens sensation. His breath comes in ever shorter, shallower gasps. He ejaculates at some point despite the pain and fear. Light bursts behind his closed, crying eyes. Before the boy passes out, he sees a beautiful cacophony of exploding stars, a collection of simultaneous supernovas.

The boy wakes up in his own bed, his mother leaning over him, one hand clutching a glass of champagne, her other cupping the boy's cheek. The windows are dark.

"Are you feeling better, baby?" his mother asks. "Did you have a nice nap? Dinner's about ready. I could use your help."

. . . .

You may never definitively be able to say whether that dream represents a true memory or not, although you've experienced some version of it at least once a month for as long as you can remember, with increased frequency in the months since you outed your stepfather. And when you experience that dream, its aftermath affects you for days, causing phantom pain in your rectum and sometimes alarming amounts of anal bleeding.

During the mornings that follow those fitful dreams, as you sit on the toilet and finally give up trying to stanch your bleeding with toilet paper, allowing your blood to spill into the water beneath you, you can't close your eyes without seeing that cacophony of exploding stars. Those simultaneous supernovas bursting inside your eyelids, conjuring the refrain of that ubiquitous, ridiculous nineties anthem, "Champagne Supernova." And you laugh and cry out those lyrics as you bleed, wondering whether you might faint.

As your psychosomatic symptoms worsen, you finally decide to see a doctor. After the most honest conversation about your sexual history you've ever attempted to have, the doctor performs a colonoscopy. The test reveals scarring in your rectum consistent with anal penetration.

This you can definitively say: you have never had sex with another man. You vaguely remember some moments of intimacy with other boys you encountered as a teenager, but nothing that approached sex. Because you could never allow the slightest sexual contact with another man, even if you wanted to. The very thought is anathema to you, immediately conjuring images of your stepfather that make you physically ill. Impossible.

You decide to stop worrying about your spotty memories. You decide to accept what you've always known. You decide to call your stepfather what he is: a rapist.

THE TABLE

AS MENTIONED, your grandfather's name is Joseph. Your grandmother's name is Josephine, of course, and Grandma never reverted
to her maiden name after their divorce. Twenty-five years later, both
of your grandparent's names remain Joe Miller. And yes, Grandma insists on the *e*.

It's Thanksgiving 1995. In three months nearly to the day, you will
turn eighteen. You identify your seat at the long, white-clothed table
laden with obscene amounts of food. Turkey and ham each hide under
silver domes, surrounded by their exposed accompaniments. Two big
bowls of salad, one Caesar and the other mixed greens; two bowls of
potatoes, one mashed, one roasted; two bowls of stuffing, one oyster,
one sausage; platters of Brussels sprouts, asparagus, and sweet potatoes are all interspersed among several boats of gravy and baskets of
bread. And there is the obligatory manicotti, essential to any Italian
Thanksgiving. But this chilled version, prepared by your Swedish stepmother, flouts tradition. It's stuffed with gin-cured gravlax, capers,
and dill crème fraiche, a sort of *fuck you, marinara* appetizer meant to
be eaten in thinly sliced bites on lightly toasted ciabatta before the real
carnage ensues.

Your seat is equidistant from each head of the table, at which captain's chairs will soon be occupied by your hosts: Great Uncle Nick,
your grandmother's older brother, and his wife, Shirley, more often
called Aunt Squirrelly. An opulent Tiffany chandelier hangs overhead,
dimly illuminating the food, the table, and the oppressive Asian antiques that surround it.

Four seats stretch to either side of yours, each indicating its intended occupant with a tasteful name card, none yet occupied. Twenty people, almost all of whom share your blood, will soon fill them. And then the game will begin.

The game involves laying bets on who will start the first argument of the evening. Normally, your father and his cousins, the Romanos, would create something similar to a football or basketball spread, a gambling chart based on the table's seating assignments, complete with arrows indicating where potential disagreements might erupt along with corresponding odds. The back of the chart would list statistics based on family dinners stretching back years. Generally, your grandmother and her brother represent the most dependable odds. A ten-dollar buy-in might return two-to-one on Grandma and Uncle Nick, ranging to five-to-one for more surprising battles.

Should any argument drive Uncle Nick to enough of a rage that his glass eye pops out, an admittedly rare but documented occurrence, there would be a jackpot. "Giarritta Powerball," your father calls it. In such an event, the first person to shout, *winner, winner, chicken dinner!* in his best racist Chinese accent wins the jackpot, with the understanding that he'll likely be banished from Uncle Nick's house for some time.

This Thanksgiving, Grandma and Uncle Nick get an early start. In fact, the chart isn't yet complete when the argument breaks out in the kitchen as dinner is still being prepared. You've always relished these arguments, but the kitchen is crowded, making the ensuing melee difficult to follow. You volunteer to put out the food, taking the opportunity to escape to the privacy of the dining room while it remains empty. The argument and its participants will follow soon enough.

Wine is displayed on a nearby buffet, a black, lacquered Chinese piece depicting snarling red dragons biting at its door handles, its surface crowded with cheap magnums: Fetzer chardonnay and merlot, Beringer white zinfandel, a few bottles of hard liquor, and a few special wines from Uncle Nick's cellar. Aunt Squirrelly, thankfully a dedicated Virginia Slim chain-smoker, has placed cut crystal ashtrays between each seat, despite the nonsmoking guests' outnumbering the smokers. You abandon your Coca-Cola for a glass of merlot, hoping that your elders are already too drunk and too involved in their fighting to notice.

Moments later, they enter. Your grandmother is destined for the seat immediately to your left. As expected, her argument with her brother continues as they lead the others to the table. You pull her chair out and she sits, barely acknowledging your presence as you tuck her in. Your grandfather takes the seat on your right, followed by your step-mother and then your father down toward Squirrelly's end of the table. You take your own seat, grateful that no one has remarked on your full wine glass or your cigarette.

Your father and his two closest cousins gave each other nicknames in their youth that they still employ when reunited, and one of them has altered each of their place cards accordingly. Charles, the likely culprit, is called Wee-Wu; Wu for short. His younger brother, Tony, is Roach. Your father is alternately called Minnow or The Mighty Min, depending on the seriousness of the context. You've never been made privy to their meanings, but eventually you concluded that Tony's moniker must refer to his pot-smoking habit. You wonder whether he'll light a joint at the table this year. Once, perhaps in an attempt to induce the Giarritta Powerball, he did so, and after he passed his joint to you, succeeded. If the opportunity presents, you resolve to be the first to yell, *winner, winner, chicken dinner*, regardless of the jackpot or consequences. What's a little bigotry if it helps solidify your place in this new family of yours? You can hope.

The cousins also share responsibility for naming Aunt Squirrelly, as well as assigning similarly cruel monikers to her daughters from her first marriage. Sherry Dawn takes the seat opposite yours, and you recall that she is actually known as Scary Dawn, a nod to her affected hippieness and new-agey ideals. Scary's sister, Gina, doesn't need a nickname. Her given name is simply pronounced to rhyme with vagina. Apparently Gina was particularly popular among the boys early in Uncle Nick's relationship with Squirrelly, before they were married. Legend tells of an illicit tryst between Roach and Gina, but as Grandma often says, "Tony was never one to let the truth get in the way of a good story." Now Gina's husband, their children, and assorted other visiting cousins fill the remaining chairs.

"Gimme a light, honey," your grandmother paws at your elbow. You dutifully light her long brown cigarette as she continues arguing with Uncle Nick. You suddenly realize that you and your own name are now, in fact, the subject of their argument.

"No, Nicky, he wasn't named after you. His name is Dominic. Nothing to do with Nicholas. Totally different name. You can't blame him if he doesn't want to be called Nick, for crissakes. He doesn't like it, and why should he?"

"For gawd's sakes, Joe, I'm not saying he has to go by Nick, I'm just saying that he was named after me, that's all. I mean, if it wasn't for me, he would've been aborted. It's like a reverse derivative. Christ, what are you, stupid?"

"Stupid," your grandmother chuckles, a hoarse, disdainful sound emitted through a cloud of smoke. "I'm the stupid one?" She turns to you, patting your leg under the table. "I love your name, Dominic. Best thing your father ever did."

"Thanks a lot, Ma," your father mutters from your right, perhaps not expecting Grandma to hear.

"Oh, shut up, Billy," your grandmother immediately turns her ire on your father. Just as quickly, she switches her attention to you, her voice softening. "What's a reverse whatever, anyways, Dominic?"

"I love his name too!" Uncle Nick shouts from the head of the table, eyes, real and false, bulging alarmingly. "Not that any of you appreciates the significance!"

Minnow, Roach, and Wu all snap their heads toward Uncle Nick, anticipating the Powerball. Your grandmother lets out another smoky chuckle, her unanswerable question forgotten. You hold your breath, ready.

"Pass the manicotti, please, Nick," Aunt Squirrelly calls, annoyed by the inauspicious start to her carefully planned meal. Uncle Nick makes a visible effort to control himself, blinking furiously, and takes a piece of manicotti before passing the platter.

The table responds to Aunt Squirrelly's tone and quiets as everyone situates themselves with food and drink. Roach folds his nametag into a paper plane and tosses it your way. It lands on your plate, in a pile of gravy-soaked mashed potatoes. You retrieve it and find a message written inside: Got any reefer, kid?

He winks at you, smiling. You shrug and smile back.

Down the table to your right, you overhear Aunt Squirrelly complimenting your stepmother, "I just love what you did with the manicotti, Jaye. I get so sick of Italian food."

Suddenly your grandfather, who you've studiously ignored, leans across your chest, laying his arm on your shoulders and sticking his painfully tilted face in front of yours, as close to your grandmother as he can manage. He smells like dried apricots. You cringe, but there's nowhere to retreat.

"Hi, Joe," he says.

The table instantly stills, all attention focused on your long-divorced grandparents and your uncomfortable seat between. Uncle Nick's good eye narrows, his Swedish manicotti propped on its slice of bread before his mouth, waiting. Your grandmother allows a few moments to pass, perhaps hoping for some distraction, any excuse to avoid your grandfather.

Finally, she responds:

"Hi, Joe."

STATUTES

IN LATE 2011, you learn that Connecticut boasts one of the most progressive statute of limitation laws in the nation concerning child sexual abuse. Victims have thirty years from the date of their eighteenth birthday to press criminal charges, file a civil suit, or both against their abuser.

That statute became law in 2003. The civil statute was made retroactive, essentially stating that anyone under age forty-eight at the time of the law's passage could sue their abuser, regardless of when the abuse occurred. Cases involving offenders at all sorts of institutions — churches, hospitals, and prep schools among them — that could not otherwise have been tried were brought to court as a direct result of the law's passage, benefiting hundreds of victims.

Unfortunately, the criminal statute was not made retroactive. Before 2003, the statute was seven years from the last known date of abuse, a figure comparable to the vast majority of other states' statutes, representing a mind-boggling loophole.

Do you remember what day it was the last time you were abused?

LEGACY

YOUR GRANDMOTHER employed a number of clichés when describing her loved ones. Tony, of course, "never let the truth get in the way of
a good story." Your father was a "bullshitter extraordinaire," a reference
also sometimes applied to you when she caught you in a lie, although
in your case, it was generally delivered with something like pride. Uncle
Nick earned her most venomous criticism: "He's a jack-of-all-trades
and a master of none, Dominic. Don't be like *him*."

Uncle Nick's pathology practice never quite commanded his full attention. He often dabbled, often disastrously, in projects ranging from
commodities trading, importing, and commercial real estate to specu-
lative sculpture commissions and regional theater productions. And
then there was his true love, a sprawling, two-story restaurant of two
hundred seats, senselessly called The Bistro.

The Bistro employed nearly every member of the family at one time
or another through the seventies and eighties. Each of the Romanos
took a turn as servers, bartenders, and cooks during their college years.
Your grandmother kept the books, a skill she acquired after her divorce,
and occasionally played hostess with legendary results. Apparently
Grandma refused to leave her cocktail or her cigarette behind while
retrieving waiting guests from the bar to seat them. Grandma often
tamped her cigarette on the guest's bread plates, mistaking them for
ashtrays. She also frequently left her lipstick-rimmed cocktail on the
table, subsequently walking off with one of the guest's drinks. When
her next sip revealed her error, her natural inclination was to accuse the
unlucky guest of stealing her drink.

Even your mother put in a stint as a cocktail waitress in the years before her brief marriage to your father, who ultimately ended up managing the whole operation while he learned how to be an alcoholic.

Uncle Nick retired in the early nineties, closing his pathology practice, cutting his losses on his various investments, and finally selling off The Bistro after years of operating in the red. He lived another two decades after retiring, and despite his poor financial choices, he managed to leave something of a legacy. His name remains proudly displayed on bronze plaques affixed to a number of buildings and sculptures throughout Cumberland. The Cumberland Regional Theatre, in particular, eventually earned a respectable reputation, although no income to speak of. Perhaps his most lasting legacy, however, can be found in his nephews, who translated portions of his passions into their own lives.

Wee-Wu, ever the practical one, followed Uncle Nick's footsteps most directly, attending medical school on the GI Bill after somehow surviving Vietnam. He became an oncologist and set up practice in upstate New York, wisely preferring to enjoy restaurants rather than operate them. His brother, Roach, however, moved to the Caribbean shortly after college. Roach opened a small classic Sicilian restaurant on Saint Thomas, appropriately named Romano's. He operated it for three decades with significant success despite his utter lack of capacity for financial management. Saint Thomas's flood of winter tourists kept Romano's predictably packed every night for six months of each year. Roach shut down altogether during the summer, spending the season's profits on any number of follies, most of them involving young women. Sometimes he went on safari.

Your father, The Mighty Min, preferred Cumberland for some unknowable reason. After years spent managing The Bistro, he opened his own restaurants with your stepmother, Jaye. Tivoli, a little lunch café that served the ever-dwindling business clientele of downtown Cumberland, doubled as the staging kitchen for their catering business. Their flagship restaurant, the Oxford House, was a hybrid Continental affair in a constant state of identity crisis, unable to decide whether it was French, Italian, German, or Swedish from day to day. The menu largely depended on your stepmother's mercurial moods.

Between Cumberland's shrinking professional population, the restaurant's lack of defined mission, and the incredible debt your father managed to accumulate, their business ultimately failed in 2011. Thankfully, both Uncle Nick and your grandmother were too far gone to dementia by that time to participate in the situation. But during the bankruptcy proceedings, as your father delved deep into his vodka while suffering through the loss of his house, his restaurants, even his Mustangs, you often heard Grandma's voice in your head: "You see, Dominic? What did I tell you? Bullshitter extraordinaire. It was bound to catch up eventually. Nicky should never have involved my son in his damned restaurant."

Uncle Nick certainly would have powerballed, but you doubt that anyone would have taken the opportunity to call, *winner, winner, chicken dinner.*

And you found yourself, at thirty-three years old, finally grateful, finally enjoying the love and support of parents no longer distracted by their business, finally able to put aside the awkward apathy of your teenage years, finally treating your parents as parents as you set about doing the hardest thing you'd ever imagined: bringing that other parent, your stepfather, to justice.

DISCOVERY

YOU'VE ACTUALLY always had a fairly good idea of when your abuse ended, but that knowledge has long been useless. You would have had to press charges against your stepfather before turning nineteen to pursue criminal prosecution.

But all is not lost. You're still protected by the civil statute, and although a lawsuit won't put your stepfather in jail or even force him to register as a sex offender, you take comfort knowing that a public civil trial will destroy his teaching career. Your chief concern since exposing your stepfather has been to keep him from working with children ever again.

By 2011, your mother and stepfather have long since left their jobs at the school where you grew up a faculty brat behind, but they both still teach at prep schools in northwestern Connecticut, your mother art, your stepfather music. Finally freed from campus living when Grandma signed over her home, your stepfather is no longer constrained to regular employment at a single school. Now he contracts with half a dozen schools across the region as well as a number of after-school arts programs.

Your mother holds a full-time job at a junior prep school, a boarding school for children aged ten through fifteen just down the road from Hotchkiss, so they can maintain a regular paycheck and health insurance. Your stepfather teaches there too.

When your mother asked for a year to consider what she would do with the knowledge of your abuse at her husband's hands, your rage was nearly uncontrollable. Gozer wanted to be heard. How could she continue sleeping under the same roof as that monster, even for a day? How could she allow him to continue teaching?

But your childhood taught you to take great care when expressing your emotions, anger in particular. It's too easy to misappropriate, and frankly you've been too emotionally volatile to trust that you would give all that anger to the right person. After all, Gozer is always near, always clamoring to be heard. You can't realistically evaluate your sanity.

So like a good little faculty brat, you follow instructions. Your new teachers live in self-help books, a leaning tower of them stacked near your bedside. You allow yourself to feel your anger, you express it through writing in your journal, and you give yourself plenty of time to calm down after the initial shock. You remind yourself again and again of how much time it took you to tell.

You allow your mother her year. Truly, you still need at least some of that time yourself.

You finally feel ready as 2011 comes to a close. It's only then that you learned that you, along with any other children of Connecticut who experienced childhood sexual abuse more than seven years before 2003, are exempt from the new criminal statute. You try to imagine bringing criminal charges against your stepfather at eighteen years old, still practically a faculty brat. It is unimaginable.

Just before Christmas you contact an attorney well known in Connecticut for trying several high-profile civil cases brought by victims of child sexual abuse, including cases at prep schools such as those where your stepfather still teaches. The lawyer impresses you with her responsiveness and compassion. She spends hours on the phone with you the first time you speak, and even reads a large portion of your journals while considering your case.

She explains that for your case to proceed, she will require the support of a larger firm. The expenses involved in such litigation go well beyond the attorney's fees. There will be forensic psychiatric evaluations for both you and your stepfather, expert witnesses, depositions, polygraphs. Preparing the lawsuit will involve an initial outlay of cash running into tens of thousands of dollars and could easily go beyond.

The lawyer's small private practice can't absorb such expenses alone, but she has a relationship with a larger Hartford firm with which she's partnered in the past in similar situations. She is positive, assuring you that your case is important and has real merit.

She is also clear on the point that to take the case, the firm will need to be reasonably certain that it can recoup the necessary expenses. Even if the attorneys involved agree to give their time pro bono, which she assures you is practically a given, the monetary award resulting from the lawsuit will have to be enough to cover all the discovery, the necessary preparation. She agrees to arrange a meeting with a partner at the Hartford law firm in February.

Just before the new year, your mother travels to Vermont to visit you and your sisters. You tell her that you're investigating a lawsuit against her husband so that he will finally be widely exposed and unable to teach. You tell her that the process has already begun. If she stays with her husband, she should prepare to go down with him, to lose her house, to lose her job, to have her name made public as the wife of a known pedophile. Or, she can leave him.

She begs you not to do it. When she realizes that you're committed, she begs you to wait, to give her more time. The tone of terror in her voice disgusts you. Your unwillingness to give her more time disgusts you. That you should be in this situation disgusts you. But you've already given her a year.

TRANSMUTATION

IN EARLY FEBRUARY, a few weeks before turning eighteen, you inform your father that you intend to move out. You've secured a roommate, a slightly older friend familiar to your family who graduated from high school a year earlier. You will rent a downtown apartment owned by your girlfriend's parents, who offered a few months of free rent in exchange for some painting and maintenance work. The apartment is nearly equidistant from school and the Oxford House, an easy walk to each. This new living situation will eliminate your father's constant annoyance at needing to chauffeur you from home, several miles outside of Cumberland proper, to your regular downtown destinations: the restaurant, where you alternate between roles as busboy, dishwasher, and prep cook, and school, where you are currently failing miserably. But your father doesn't need to know that.

Nor does he need to know that your girlfriend, already in college, lives in the apartment below the one you'll share with your new roommate. Or that the three of you will, in effect, share the entire space. More specifically, your father doesn't need to know that this entire plan is mostly a ploy that will allow you to share your girlfriend's bed at will.

Thankfully, your father never expresses particular interest in the details of your sex life, but he does have strong opinions concerning unplanned pregnancy. You feel certain that, given the complete context of your decision, he would rightly conclude that your plan represents an exponential increase of that risk and flatly refuse to allow it.

Twenty months have passed since you left Connecticut. This time represents the most transformative period of your short life. Your Maryland family is now, simply, your family, an inversion representative of your successful separation from your former home. You already find it difficult to remember the mindset of your slightly younger self, that perpetually petrified, broken boy desperate to escape his step-father. The shock of freedom that boy experienced the day he boarded the train in New Haven has mutated into an expectation to which you now feel entitled.

You even find yourself chafing against the relatively loose constraints of your father's attempted parenting, his willingness to allow far more freedom than most of your school friends enjoy, tempered only by his insistence that you avoid premature fatherhood, work regularly, and his stern promise that, should you ever be arrested, he will allow you to spend the night in jail.

Your friends envy your lack of curfew, the late weeknights and even later weekend nights made possible by your father's workaholic, alcoholic schedule. They're even jealous of your job, the evening shifts that end with wine and Belgian ale "tastings" provided by waiters and cooks whose greatest pleasure seems to be corrupting the boss's kid. And on nights when you're free from work, you're largely free to do as you please. At least until your father makes his drunken way home, generally somewhere between midnight and two in the morning. You sometimes manage to miss even that fluid curfew, arriving home shortly before dawn on your bicycle or in a friend's car, creeping into the house to find your father snoring, passed out on the couch in front of the television with a tumbler and an empty liter of vodka on the nearby coffee table. When he finally wakes up, a few moments of conversation will confirm that he remembers little of the previous night, including whether you'd been home.

Despite your relative teenage freedom, you want more. You've become a junkie, ruled by an insatiable craving for independence, the complete absence of oversight. Even the loosest constraints are too tight. So you inform your father that you're moving out. You make it clear that you are not asking for his permission. He surprises you by promptly giving it.

With one condition: your father and stepmother have planned a rare vacation this February, the restaurant's slowest month of the year, right around the time of your birthday. They will spend two weeks in California, visiting family and "tasting" wine. Their intention was to bring you along, but if you're planning to move out, your father informs you, you might as well stay behind. He'd be happy to save the airfare.

They've planned care for your ancient grandfather, but again, your father continues, if you're staying behind, you might as well make yourself useful and see to your grandfather yourself. You will have use of your stepmother's Subaru. You will pick up your grandfather's prepared meals from the restaurant, deliver them, and clean up after him each day. You will *not* drive your father's lovingly restored Mustang under any circumstances. You will not miss any school, and although you haven't been scheduled for work during those weeks, you will make yourself available as needed, even if that means working on your birthday. And you will feed the cats and Truman, the dog who became your closest friend in the months immediately following your arrival in Cumberland.

Thrilled by the idea that you'll have exclusive use of a car for two weeks, you promptly agree. Your father quietly regards you, his expression slightly amused, slightly dubious. He's never trusted your lack of interest in his Mustang.

"Are you sure?" he asks. "This trip was going to be your birthday present."

"Yes," you answer. "I'm sure."

"If you drive my Mustang, I'll know. I'll have you arrested, and you can spend a night in jail."

"I won't touch the Mustang."

"Okay then. Good. Do *not* fuck this up."

You have no intention of fucking this up, especially after your father becomes astonishingly cooperative in the days leading up to your move. He replaces your planned birthday present with gifts of handed-down but perfectly serviceable furniture: a queen-sized bed, a couch, a dining set, kitchenwares and utensils from the restaurant, even a huge television that requires more hands to move than the couch. He sends employees and the catering van to help with the large items on moving day and later sends them back laden with sandwiches and your favorite Belgian ales.

"Your dad is the *coolest*," your new roommate declares, after washing down a mouthful of muffuletta with a swig of Corsendonk.

You're not at all certain that your dad is the coolest. In all these months you've lived with him, despite all the years spent wishing for him, you have yet to feel comfortable calling him Dad. You've had no trouble settling into relationships with other members of your new family, your grandmother, your aunts and uncles, even your stepmother, all of whom have accepted your presence naturally, all of whom you've accepted with equal ease.

But you've been unable to achieve even remotely similar ease with your father, the relationship that matters most, and you've been unable to identify why. Is it your own hesitation? Is it his? Why should either of you hesitate? Perhaps it's his alcoholism, of which you've only recently become fully aware.

Whatever the reason, in this moment, sipping your favorite beer, recovering from the not unpleasant ache of your labor, enjoying a wonderful new sense of freedom and ownership as you sit on the floor of your first apartment, the first space that's ever truly been yours, you cannot bring yourself to disagree with your roommate. Perhaps your dad is the coolest. Perhaps you're responsible for the awkwardness between you.

Two weeks later, with a few days remaining before your father returns from California, you find yourself slacking on your agreement. There's no practical reason for it. The meal delivery and cleanup doesn't take more than two hours out of your day. You've got the car. You haven't been called into work. The Oxford House cooks prepare your grandfather's meals every morning, much more than the Oldest of Men, as the staff calls him, could ever consume in a day. They faithfully keep your delivery ready for your arrival after school. All you have to do is pick the meals up, return any dirty dishes from the previous day to the restaurant, steal a few of those delicious Belgian beers, and head home to your new apartment right up the street.

You keep the schedule religiously during the first days of your new life in your new apartment, making your deliveries, feeding the pets, and taking Truman for a three-mile run on the hard-packed snow, his favorite activity. You even water your stepmother's plants when they look wilted, a chore that makes you feel particularly adult. Then you shower and change before returning your grandfather's dirty dishes to the restaurant.

But each time you visit, your grandfather seems to want more from you, demanding that you spend time with him and make conversation in a way he never attempts in your father's presence. He wants to know why you moved out, he wants to know about your grandmother, he wants to know how you're doing in school, why you feel the need to bathe so often, and why you spoil the dog.

Most important, he wants to make sure that you aren't too distracted by girls. He repeatedly tells you the story about how, when he felt sexually frustrated as a young man, all he had to do was pay three dollars for a blow job from any of the young Sicilian prostitutes back in Hackensack. That way, he wouldn't become distracted. Girls are trouble, he earnestly assures you, and you should do whatever you must to keep them from driving you mad.

Following your father's departure, you made your deliveries promptly at 3:30 p.m., but recently you've pushed your arrival time back an hour. Your grandfather likes to eat at five o'clock, and showing up closer to his mealtime seems to help mitigate his desire for conversation.

Today, the day that will mark your last delivery, you arrive too late. It's past Joe's dinner hour, nearly full dark. You regret missing the chance to take Truman for a run.

Lights shine from the interior of the house. Shadows project through the kitchen windows, moving oddly, fast, shuttering across the undisturbed snow. You gather your bags, one filled with plates, cutlery, and beverages, the other with stacked takeout boxes, and head for the kitchen door, skating carefully on the ice.

Inside, you find your grandfather standing over the kitchen table, hands braced against the blonde oak surface, kicking Truman where he lies curled up underneath, whimpering.

Your father rescued Truman from a kill shelter as a puppy, already too large for most people to consider adopting. He was always a big dog, some sort of sturdy Shepherd mix assumed to be an overgrown mutt. Later your father discovered a number branded inside his big, soft ear, and learned that he'd been bred in Texas specifically for border patrol. You never discovered the details of how he ended up in Cumberland, something to do with a nomadic restaurant employee.

Truman now weighs well over a hundred pounds. Your grandfather couldn't possibly outweigh him by much. You can't believe what you're seeing: your ancient, arthritic grandfather, furiously wailing away on your dog with his ridiculous, fur-slippered foot, white hair flying around his unnaturally bent neck, flopping against his shoulder as he kicks again and again. And Truman, your dog, your friend, cringing under the table, crying out in response to each blow.

Shocked, unable to speak, you throw your grandfather's food at him, slinging it at his head with all your strength. The plastic bag hits your grandfather full in the face, making an audible pop as the boxes inside explode and spill their contents over his shoulders and onto the floor around him, marinara coating the whole scene. In a surreal flash, you take particular note of Truman as he artfully grabs a fallen meatball in his jaws and gulps it down. Your grandfather shakes his head, his white hair flinging blood red sauce. He continues kicking, ignoring you. Truman yelps again.

Without another thought, you drop the other bag, noting the sound of china cracking as it hits the floor.

You tackle your grandfather, taking his midriff against your right shoulder, lifting him up and running him through the kitchen into the living room, trying to ignore the sickening thud as the back of his head bounces off the trim over the threshold. You eject him from your grasp onto the couch and stand over him, panting.

"What. The fuck. Are you doing?" you breathlessly ask.

Your grandfather cannot respond. Even in your astonished rage, you worry that you might have seriously hurt him. He remains still, splayed on the couch, the papery white flesh of his lower belly disturbingly exposed, trying to catch his breath.

Seven decades his junior, you catch your breath sooner. "What the hell is wrong with you? Why would you do that? How could you? He's just a dog. You fucking monster!"

You wait a few moments, disgusted, hoping for some explanation, immediately concluding that you don't have the stomach for any justification he might offer. Your grandfather remains unable to respond, quietly hyperventilating, his eyes closed, his right hand clutching his chest, then the back of his head, his left raised toward you, warding you off. You wonder whether you should call an ambulance.

"I hope you fucking die right there, Old Man," you say, astonished to hear your own words, instantly realizing that you mean them absolutely. You turn away from him, returning to the kitchen, where you find Truman happily lapping up the last of the meatballs meant for your grandfather.

"Come here, buddy," you say, clapping your thigh as you kneel. Truman responds immediately, abandoning his feast and giving your face a big lick before laying his neck on your shoulder, the same sort of hug he gave you when you moved into this house, twenty months ago.

"Let's get you out of here."

You leave the mess in the kitchen and take Truman to your apartment, coaxing him up onto the queen-sized bed your father gave you, trying to discern any injuries, marveling at Truman's easy acceptance as you press along his ribs as if you know what to do. He licks your prodding hand, smiling, happy, reflecting no effect of the trauma that has left you with trembling hands and soaked in sweat.

You call the restaurant to let the staff know that someone else will need to deliver meals to your grandfather for the next few days. When asked why, you promptly hang up the phone, unable to offer an explanation.

Your grandmother is the only person you really want right now, but it doesn't seem appropriate to involve her in anything to do with her hated ex-husband. After considering for some time, you finally call Uncle Nick, steeling yourself for the scolding you're sure to receive, uncharacteristically prepared to scold right back.

Uncle Nick answers his phone on the second ring, and your resolve disappears as you immediately begin to cry. You tell your story in strengthless sobs.

Uncle Nick is silent for several moments after you finish. You try to control your tears, awaiting his response, full of trepidation.

"I am so sorry, Dominic," he finally says, his normally certain, stern voice almost unrecognizable, drenched with sympathetic care. He sounds near tears himself. "I'm so sorry you had to see that. I'm going to take care of it. Is Truman okay? We'll get him to the vet first thing in the morning. And I'll talk to your father. Don't you worry about a thing. Get some rest, son. And do not go back to that house on your own."

CROSS-EXAMINATION

YOU SIT WITH YOUR mother in your sister's bright Vermont kitchen, the February sun magnified by fresh snow. It's late afternoon, getting colder outside by the moment. Your mother looks exhausted. She's aged dramatically this year. She retreats upstairs to her daughter's guest bedroom for a nap.

People who know Christina call her high-energy, just as you considered her precocious as a child, and they mean it as a compliment. She's an elementary school teacher, after all, and high-energy is a prerequisite of the job. Since you told her that her father is a pedophile and you were his victim, your relationship with your sister has changed. Recently you find her simply nervous, at least in your presence. It deeply saddens you that you've caused this change. It makes you angry that you're considered the cause.

You sit on the couch by the fire. She pours you a glass of wine, and you sip quietly together for a little while, sitting close, companionable enough. Suddenly she says, "This is just so hard on Mom. It's so hard on all of us."

You finally snap. You've tried to be so patient with your mother over the course of the year. And what Christina said is absolutely true, you recognize that truth, and in other circumstances you might even be willing to explore that truth with her, but apparently you have no reserves left for your sister.

Your voice rising uncontrollably, you ask her if she thinks this is easy on *you*. Does she think that you enjoy alienating your family? Does she think that, having told your story, you're all better now? Does she think it's easy to recall memories of rape and terrible, sometimes torturous abuse, to suffer panic attacks and crazy-making somatic symptoms, to wake up screaming after sleeping only a couple of hours, to wonder if you're losing your mind, to be utterly alone, to feel betrayed by your family?

Your sister remains uncharacteristically silent and stone-faced throughout your litany. You are forcibly reminded of her father at his angriest, and the realization takes your breath away. You stop talking and stand up, gathering your things, simply unable to be in the same room with her.

As you prepare to leave, one more question occurs to you.

"Do you prioritize the welfare of your family over the safety of children?"

"Yes," she answers. "And you are a part of that family."

She said, "Yes." Your sister. The elementary school teacher with the ideal Vermont life who just happened to be fathered by a pedophile answered, "Yes."

You bundle up and head for the door.

Your mother comes down the stairs just as you're about to exit the house.

"Wait a minute, baby," she says, and something in her tone makes you hope. You turn and wait.

She stands just above you on the stairs. She wraps her arms around you and holds you for a long moment.

Your stepfather is two hundred miles away, and you haven't had any contact with him for a full calendar year. Your rapist is finally expelled from your life, but you can offer no clearer picture of the horrible dilemma of the abusive home than this moment shared with your mother. It feels so good to be held by her that way, standing on the step above you, holding your head to her breast. You'd been without the benefit of loving human touch for months, and this is your mother. You want to be able to enjoy that contact, to lean into it, to take strength.

And with her next words, she makes it impossible.

"I just need to ask you one more time to reconsider. Please." And then, "I'm blameless in all of this. Please think of what I've been through."

As you absorb her words, you no longer have the energy for rage. In that moment, all you are capable of feeling is the most profound sadness. But you cannot allow your deep need for comfort or your sadness to influence your behavior. You cannot afford compromise. You cannot lean on your mother.

Your rage understands this, Gozer understands. He will not be pushed aside after hearing those words. Gozer seizes control, relishing in pure indignation as he sends his anger forth, out through your limbs and into your hands.

Gozer backs away from your mother, takes her by the shoulders, and turns her down the hall, harshly, gutturally instructing, "Come on," propelling her toward the couch where your sister—your *half* sister— still sits.

Since that teenage incident with your grandfather, you've never manhandled anyone so, and this is your mother, but Gozer knows just what to do. For a brief moment, Gozer is no longer distinguishable from yourself. Your mother starts to protest, but you cut her off. "No, Mom," you say. "I need you both to hear this."

Your mother falls to the couch next to your sister, and you stand above them, already sweating in your winter gear, already thankfully (regrettably) feeling that sudden, shocking surge of Gozer rage dissipate.

"Do you understand what you're asking of me?" you fight the tears and fail. The rest comes out in maddeningly disjointed croaks, just like your most maddening recurring dreams, those in which you can never quite say exactly what you need to say, let alone throw a solid punch. But you do the best you can, desperate to be heard.

"You're asking me to choose our family's comfort over the safety of children. You are asking me to bury everything that happened to me, to forget it *again*. You are asking me to choose our fucked family over what is clearly right."

And then directly to your mother, "When the choice between right and wrong is so clear, how can you ask me to choose what is wrong— morally wrong? You're my mother," you force the words out as best you can, breathless, disembodied, certain that all of this is real but unable

148

to ignore that twinge of doubt, hyperaware and hyperdisturbed by the heavy, dreamlike quality weighing down on you and muddying your thoughts as you vocalize them, making your words feel strange in your mouth.

Finally finished, you wait for your mother and your sister, for either of them to respond, but they don't until you turn to leave yet again.

Then they come after you, stopping you at the front door. They hold you tight and assure you that they support you, and you allow it, although no part of you believes them.

Your sister's words come easily, clearly, with no hesitation. She says many things but all you will remember is her reiteration, "I value our family above all things, and you are part of that."

Your mother says, "I just want you to be happy again, baby."

MISNOMERS

RESTAURANTS OF ALL SORTS, from the humblest burger joint to the loftiest fine dining venue, share a remarkable degree of consistency in the behavior of their staffs. Giving nicknames is a perfect example. For instance, your father's and his cousin's nicknames come from The Bistro.

Uncle Nick's restaurant legacy continued beyond Roach and Minnow, extending into your own life as you came of working age. Which is how you find yourself, in your early twenties, managing that bougie hotel restaurant where you served the Buccelli family, repeating the habits of your father, naming your own group of restaurant comrades.

Your assistant, Tamara, is a recent refugee from a nudist resort just over the border in West Virginia, where her uniform consisted of only an apron and a pair of Dansko clogs. Sometimes a hairnet. You call her Tam-Nation.

Shannon, an annoyingly handsome, perfectly formed gay waiter who sleeps with at least as many women as men but would never consider identifying as bisexual, is Shan-Lon. You're not sure that anyone could say why. Sometimes his full name, Shan-Lon B. Johnson, seems more appropriate. Often, after too much wine, it devolves to Johnson B. Johnson, then simply Johnson. The three of you are very close.

Shane, a busboy, is Sha-nay with the Man Ass, an acknowledgment of his remarkably formed bubble butt, or simply Sha-nay-nay. Shan-Lon often says of Sha-Nay-Nay, "I think that's what they mean when men say 'she's got the ass of a twelve-year-old boy.' I know he's not twelve or anything, but they do say that, right? Isn't that weird? I've always thought that was a little weird. Until Sha-Nay came along, anyway. Now I kind of get it."

Vincent, a fellow half-breed Italian who works as a line cook, is blessed with an intriguingly strong-featured face and a positively sensual mouth that's earned him the name Vincent with the Man Lips. Vincenzo for short, or simply Vincenz.

Ashley, a ninety-pound waitress with an oversized bosom and a pill addiction, is called Trashley, more out of respect for her love of anal sex than hard drugs.

"I mean, pussy's pussy, you know what I mean?" Trashley often announces with little or no context, her Valley girl accent augmented by a distinctive nasal quality, the result of a crushed-Klonopin and cocaine-eroded septum. "When I *really* want a guy, I give him the *butt*."

Eventually Shan-Lon's teenage nephew, Andrew, joins the crew as a busboy, and you dub him Andrew with All of the Hotness of Shan-Lon and None of the Gay. Shan-Lon and Tam-Nation call you Dominatrix, sometimes simply 'Natrix. You are the manager, after all.

"My dick, your mouth," Shan-Lon greets you at the beginning of each dinner service.

"No, my dick, *your* mouth," is your standard response before calling the nightly service meeting to order.

Overhearing your exchange, Trashley often interjects, "You can do that at the same time, you know. It doesn't have to be either-or. I mean, sixty-nine, hello?" Your corporate bosses have instructed you to develop a team mentality in your staff, an annoyingly nebulous concept your father's lessons didn't directly address. But perhaps you've succeeded after all.

One night, while finishing up the evening's service and drinking cheap sauvignon blanc from a repurposed iced tea dispenser in the waiter's area, Trashley makes the error of calling Shan-Lon's nephew Andrew with all of the Hotness of Shan-Lon *but* None of the Gay. Perhaps replacing *and* with *but* represents a Freudian slip related to her well-known love of butt. Perhaps Andrew's new name is simply too long. Either way, Shan-Lon feels the need to correct her on the importance of the distinction.

"It's *and* None of the Gay, not *but*," Shan-Lon scolds.

"Seriously? What's the difference?" she asks, always so earnest.

Shan-Lon lacks the patience to answer, shaking his head as he dispenses more wine, waving at you to respond.

"But implies a negative connotation to being gay," you explain. "It's a subtle difference, but important."

"Do you get that?" Shan-Lon asks.

"Yeah," Trashley answers. "Yeah, I do get it. Andrew with all of the Hotness of Shan-Lon *and* None of the Gay. And it's totally true, but seriously, you guys, it's too long. I can't yell all that at him when I need him to bus my tables or fuck my ass, you know what I mean?"

You and Shannon are nearly always the last to leave work, your conversations and the lure of free wine complementing your lack of interest in returning home to your wife, often keeping you from doing so for hours after closing. Somehow, your exchange with Ashley spirals into a much deeper conversation than usual. Shannon is one of the very few people you'll remember sharing your secret with in your twenties.

You do so only in the broadest strokes. You don't intend to be purposefully vague with him, in fact you trust him completely, but you aren't yet prepared to speak frankly about your childhood under any circumstances.

Thankfully, Shannon isn't particularly interested in the gory details of the repeated rapes you endured as a child. He's more concerned with your current mindset, the lasting consequences that, he points out, are noticeable to anyone close enough to see once the context is provided.

"I know you hear this all the time from redneck assholes around here," he says, earnest as Ashley in his way. "I hope this doesn't offend you, but I have to say that I've always wondered if you really might be gay. I know you're married, of course, but I've had plenty of lovers who were married to women. And, you know, the vast majority of their wives have no idea. Or at least if they do, they never say anything. Have you ever felt like you might be gay?"

"Always," you gush, astonished by how good it feels to confess. You've never done so, to anyone. "At least while I was a teenager. I mean, I had gay sex as a child. For years. I certainly didn't want it, but I'd be lying if I said it didn't feel good sometimes. Parts of it, at least. And then, while I was a teenager, I had a few encounters with boys. Nothing particularly physical, I don't think. Mostly at raves, high on ecstasy or whatever else was put in front of me. I barely remember any of it. But then I got married, and I just never gave it much thought after that."

Shannon encourages you to speak freely, and you do. You tell him about your inability to anticipate circumstances that might make you feel sexual discomfort, suddenly panicked and unable to perform or identify why. How these episodes ended many of your young relationships in embarrassment and confusion. How your marriage seems to work only because it's largely sexless, and your ever-growing fear that it isn't, in fact, working at all. How you love Shannon himself deeply, and how you've certainly loved other men and boys before him. How you feel utterly repulsed by the thought of the slightest sexual contact with any man. How you thought that you might, in fact, have been born gay, or at least bisexual, but that your stepfather had taken that possibility from you forever.

How you will never know.

CLOSING ARGUMENT

YOU'RE DRIVING THROUGH northwestern Connecticut, taking the long way to Hartford along old, intimately familiar roads. You've been tuned into midday NPR for four hours and haven't heard a word. Instead, that damn Harry Nilsson song from *The Point!*, "Me and My Arrow," keeps flitting through your head, the same refrain, again and again, a maddeningly silly mantra hijacking your every wayward thought.

In the song, Arrow refers to pointless Oblio's dog, his constant companion during his banishment in the Pointless Forest. Like Skye, your old black Lab from childhood. Now you envision your arrow more literally, a sharp spear of righteous indignation.

It's Valentine's Day 2012. In ten days, you will turn thirty-four years old. You have very little idea of what to expect from this very important meeting with very important lawyers about the source of all your bitterness. You take some comfort from the knowledge that your own lawyer will be there, the nice lady who read your journals and immediately declared herself *your* lawyer, although you haven't paid her a dime.

You're driving through northwestern Connecticut even though it puts you more than an hour out of your way. But you've needed that hour, because you left Vermont at least two hours too early. You're having trouble identifying your feelings, but you understand that the intense blend of anxiety and hope and optimism and cynicism rattling around your thoughts are all parts of a type of anticipation you could never possibly have anticipated.

You strive for equilibrium, and when that fails, ambivalence. You repeat this exercise again and again, your heavy breathing rhythmically matching that silly Harry Nilsson refrain, Tom Ashbrook's cultivated NPR voice blending unintelligibly just below. But as Ashbrook announces a break, reminding his audience of the name of his show, his words break through your reverie: *On Point.* You hear yourself bark, a harsh, ugly chuckle from far away.

Finally, you arrive in Hartford, and even after the parking search gave anxiety the momentary prize in your battling emotions, you're still forty minutes early. No matter, apparently. The receptionist greets you warmly and leads you to a conference room, assuring you that the schedule is easily adjusted this late in the day. They will join you shortly.

They do join you shortly, and they are as expected. You met them all when you were still a faculty brat, which suddenly doesn't seem so long ago.

Your lawyer is the benevolent art teacher, one of the few among her colleagues who doesn't mind your making a mess of the ceramic studio or the photo lab. Another lawyer is an administrator, sternly confident but deferring to his better. His better is a student's parent, too busy manifesting success to bother with a display of confidence or concern about anyone else in the room, including you.

You suddenly, shockingly, assume complete control of your faculties. All your clamoring emotions are immediately, forcefully quieted, and what remains is something like the ambivalence you sought earlier, but more. Dissociation. You gratefully accept the calm that comes with it, acknowledging that this is exactly what you need. You sink into that (absence of) feeling, visualizing its protection, a shining suit of medieval armor that will keep all the dangers of the world well removed from your flesh. You imagine yourself slamming shut the steel visor on your helm, masking your face.

Besides your lawyer, there is one other woman in the room, an unknown quantity who sits opposite the attorneys, on your side of the table but six chairs down. You decide she is the headmaster. The parent may supersede her, but she exudes a similar sense of detached superiority. Is she wearing armor as well? You realize that's your cynicism talking. You hope it's mistaken.

You stand for introductions and learn that you're correct in all your assumptions. The administrator is just that, a junior associate assigned to ask the questions and document your answers. The parent is a senior partner at the firm. The headmaster is someone from the state's attorney's office. Your ambivalence briefly wavers — the state's attorney. *What could her presence mean?* You banish the thought. The hope it represents is too scary, an unacceptable threat. You reimagine your armor, chain link under plate, seamless, impervious.

You're peppered with questions for exactly one hour. They begin simply enough.

"Please state your full name."

"Dominic Joseph Miller."

"Any aliases or prior names?"

"Dominic Joseph Marshall."

"The accused's full name?"

And you answer, alarmed by how easily the utterance of your step-father's full name — the accused's full name — immediately creates a chink in your armor, as if a hot poker fresh from the forge had pierced it.

From there, the questions circle inward, seeking an embarrassing degree of specificity.

"Did the accused manually stimulate your penis?"

"Yes."

"How often?"

"I can't be sure. Countless times."

"Did the accused orally stimulate your penis?"

"Yes."

"How many times?"

"I'm sorry, I don't know. Many."

"Did the accused ask you to manually stimulate his penis?"

"Yes."

"And you did so?"

"Yes."

"How many times?"

"Often, many times."

"A dozen times? A hundred?"

"At least."

"At least a dozen?"

"At least a hundred."

"Did the accused penetrate you orally with his penis?"

"Yes."

"How many times?"

"At least twice that I recall, but I think it may have happened more."

"Did the accused penetrate you anally with his penis?"

"I believe he did."

"You *believe* he did? Can you elaborate?"

And as best you can, you elaborate, describing your dreams, your psychosomatic symptoms, your doctor's determination that you had, in fact, been repeatedly anally penetrated, whether you remember it perfectly or not.

The partner apparently read the same material from the journals you sent your lawyer, although as you continue answering questions it quickly becomes clear that he hasn't done so very closely. He often interjects, often answers for you, often incorrectly. You carefully correct him every time, trying for diplomacy but feeling the ultimate imperative to maintain whatever control of this room you can. You add Odysseus's bow to your armor, complete with an enchanted, wickedly pointed arrow, a weapon of exposure, of truth, justice. You sense the lawyer's annoyance several times and finally give up caring. Your own annoyance utterly eclipses his, you're certain, although you hope that you do a better job of hiding it than he does. Even as you visualize cutting through his false words with your magical arrow.

It becomes clear to you that a decision has already been reached regarding your case, and that you are not going to like it. You spend that hour trying like hell to illustrate the desperate necessity of keeping your stepfather out of schools, away from young boys, all the while feeling your ambivalence slipping away, your armor failing. Pain, real, present, and unavoidable, insinuates itself, demanding to be felt.

Near the end of the perfectly measured hour, the partner explains to you that his firm will not be taking your case. The school where you grew up a faculty brat cannot be held culpable. You were not a student at the school, and therefore the school was not responsible for your welfare despite your having been repeatedly sexually assaulted on its campus, by one of the school's employees, in your home provided by the school.

Additionally, most unfortunately, your stepfather is simply too poor to be worth suing. Although your case is absolutely winnable, the firm cannot be reasonably assured that it will recoup the cost of pursuing it.

You realize that you've been expecting this answer almost from the moment they entered the room, but the pain accompanying the finality of hearing these words spoken aloud is still a shock. You feel it throughout your body, nausea radiating from your gut, your hands suddenly cold and clammy, your face flushed and hot. In sharp contrast to your body's confusion, your mind begins cycling through a series of practical questions, dimming the light of your mythic arrow, dispelling the last of your armor, denying the dissociation you crave. As you feel yourself sinking all the way into your painful, anxiety-ridden body, you find yourself wondering: *Why did all you very important people waste your very important time? And my own admittedly less important time?*

The headmaster, the representative of the state's attorney, who had remained silent throughout the hour, answers your question when you voice your slightly more politic version of it. She explains that even though there is no viable lawsuit, she wanted to meet you. She wanted to hear your story in person. She assures you that your stepfather will be thoroughly investigated, and if there is any evidence of current abuse, he will be brought to justice.

Dumping politic, you ask her what sort of evidence that might be. She cannot answer you. She simply says, "Now he's on our radar."

She stands as she says it, and they all follow suit. The administrator, the parent, even your benevolent teacher. Finally, you rise as well and find the parent's hand thrust in your direction. You shake his hand firmly, as you were taught—Grandpa would have been proud—while he mutters, "I'm sorry for your trouble, and I wish you the best of luck."

The headmaster has already left the room, quickly followed by the administrator. The parent follows, already on his phone, already discussing the next, more profitable legal battle. You're left with your benevolent art teacher, your lawyer, who kindly hugs you and assures you that she'll help with any advocacy information she can.

In the lobby, the receptionist chases you down the hall as you make your way to the elevator. She wants to validate your parking ticket. You left it in the car. You tell her not to worry about it, ignoring the functional part of your brain telling you, *Yes, be worried. You may not have enough gas to get home to the relative safety of Vermont.*

In the elevator, you only realize that you're crying when someone else gets on a couple of floors down. He carefully averts his eyes and you're reminded to control yourself. You exit the elevator together in the garage. The sharp, smart sound of his remote opening his spotless black BMW next to your salt-spattered Subaru startles you so badly that you begin to hyperventilate. You realize that you're on the verge of a panic attack, a sensation you've become intimate with in recent months.

You consider walking around the State Capitol, which is right across the street. It's a beautifully clear, crisp day, at least twenty degrees warmer than northern Vermont. Relatively balmy for February. It seems like a good idea, but you can't bear to be in this building, in this city, or in this state for another moment. You gingerly get into your car. Your hand is shaking badly enough that you have trouble getting your key in the ignition, and you suddenly recall the image of your grandmother, high on the pot. The thought brings no laughter.

The parking attendant demands seven dollars and fifty cents. You hand over your last crumpled bills, and somehow this brings up a laugh where even the thought of stoned Grandma could not. The attendant looks at you, interested. You don't bother explaining that this folly will end up costing fifty bucks round trip, the last of all your current resources. Pretty cheap to be told that all your plans are canceled, of course, but still, it's everything you have.

Finally, you're on I-91 speeding north out of the city, out of Connecticut. No long way through the Berkshires for you this time. As you put some distance between yourself and the meeting, you realize that you're barely in control, and the slightest surprise could send you skid-ding or flipping down the highway at seventy-five miles per hour. You should pull off for a bit. Try to find ambivalence again, the safety of that dissociative state, that place in which you were once able to endure anything.

So you do. You pull off in some terrible suburb between Hartford and Springfield and focus on your breathing, willing your body to stillness, trying to find your armor.

But your breath won't stop hitching in your throat. You can't control it. Instead, you cry. You feel like you did when you were a faculty brat, back when you were small and absolutely convinced that you could be as loud as you wanted in the parked car and no one would hear you.

And that makes you laugh. Of course they hear you. Passersby look at you furtively on their way to Starbucks as you choke and cry and laugh and choke and cry at how unfair it all is. Your stepfather is too poor to sue. Saved by his own irresponsibility. The school can't be sued, its roster of well-paid attorneys, many of them multigenerational alumni, having somehow planned for this very situation along with any other unimaginable contingency.

You should have known. All your plans, all your threats, all your principle, meaningless. Your mother might as well stay married to him. You might as well never have told. There is no ambivalence. There is no escape. There is no justice.

You've read about "nonstarter" cases. Your recent experience with poverty provided an unexpected, important education, but the people depicted in those nonstarter stories are poor in a way you could never fully understand. They are the inner-city folk you thoughtlessly passed by as a teenager, selfishly seeking escape, the sheer pleasure of illicit drugs in Alphabet City. They are their Appalachian counterparts you encountered while doing the same in western Maryland and nearby West Virginia when you lived with your father. They represent a whole segment of unrecognized, devalued, practically discarded Americans who have been denied options, let alone dreams, from their very birth. How many of them endured something similar, something worse, even, than what you'd lived through? How many did you pass by without a thought?

While you've learned some degree of what it means to be poor, the privileges of your youth, utterly unrecognized at the time, insistently persist. You grew up in one of the wealthiest counties in America, raised in an educational tradition whose sole purpose is to produce new generations of leaders in government and industry and academia. You have dreams, even expectations, all born of and enforced by a sense of entitlement that, in retrospect, disgusts you even as it continues to inform your very existence.

And yet, you have no legal recourse. Your armor, that shining visualization of impervious dissociation, was never anything more than a romantic illusion, every bit as maddeningly silly as that Harry Nilsson song you so loved in your childhood. Your arrow is blunt, worthless, pointless.

Your stepfather got away with it. Your rapist got away with it. He will continue to wear his worn tweeds and scuffed loafers, he will continue to be respected, even beloved in the wealthy, overeducated community of your childhood, he will continue to teach young boys to play drums with their hands, and he will continue to have opportunities to destroy whole lives in a matter of moments. You cannot legally prevent this. You thought you could, it seemed so clear that you could, it was the right thing to do, and you fucking tried to do it, but you cannot.

You are not allowed.

You are a faculty brat.

III

BUCCA

The Myth of Sisyphus

ORIENTATION

IMAGINE AN AVERAGE DAY, a banal errand, navigating one of the endless necessities of modern American life.

"Hi there, thanks for choosing Jiffy Lube!" The muffled greeting penetrates your sealed car window as you pull up to the squat concrete garage, grateful to leave the congestion of Route 7 behind. You haven't even managed to roll your aging Subaru over the parking lot's black bell snake, with its universally sharp, startlingly loud "ding-ding," let alone roll your window down. *Already fucking it up,* you think.

This sort of drive-up scenario invariably causes you anxiety, these simple interactions that millions of Americans navigate millions of times each day all over the country, on thousands of stretches of highway largely identical to this one. Ordering from a fast food drive-through, approaching a car wash, donating to Goodwill, getting the oil changed: you do all of these things as rarely as possible, a choice representing one of the primary motivators in your relocation from the suburban stretches of Maryland to mostly rural Vermont in the first place, some six years ago. Back when you were closer to thirty than forty. Back when your principles were clear and relatively inviolate, easy to identify and adhere to. Back before all the complications.

But that homogenous highway exists even here in Vermont, funneling traffic toward Burlington while serving the ever-present needs of ever-needful consumers, including you. The young man attempting to greet you stands just outside your window, still closed as you fumble to turn down NPR (*no, Dominic, just turn it off*) put the car in park (but not before your foot lifts off the brake enough that the car rolls forward half a foot, resulting in another startling "ding!"), and move your hand to roll down the window (wondering, as you depress the automated button, why you persist in thinking of it as rolling anything down) before finally killing the ignition (*after putting the car in park, after, dammit*).

Oh, and you'd better put the cap back on your Coca-Cola (*you're gonna want that later, good and fizzy, with a cigarette*). Speaking of which, grab your cigarettes. Lighter. And don't forget your phone. And your book. And your wallet. Where is your wallet?

"What can we do you for today?" You stifle a wince at the volume of the Jiffy Lube guy's voice. He smiles broadly, his voice artificially brimming with energy, his uniform golf shirt like the medieval sigil of some particularly heinous feudal lord (*Alan Rickman as the Sheriff of Nottingham?*), a strip of black bisecting triangles of bilious yellow and a shade of burgundy gone to rust across his chest, all spotted with, you imagine, oil.

Knights of the Oil Republic, you think. And then, *Sir Jiffy Lube of the Order of Enthused Oil Men.*

"Um, well, I'd like an oil change, please," you say, hoping you don't sound like you're mocking him even as the contrarian in you considers, *What can we do for you, you mean? How about a dirty fucking martini?* And then, *Oh, of course. There must be choices. Options. You're such an asshole. But what are the options? Where are they?*

"Just the basic oil change, I suppose?"

"Okay, sir, that's *great*. Why don't you step out of the car? Whoops, you can leave those," gesturing to the keys still clutched in your hand. You toss them to the seat, more flustered with each moment. "Follow me, sir, I'll get you taken care of," already striding purposefully away, crossing the parking lot to the front door. "This Door to Remain OPEN During Business Hours," reads a slightly askew sticker stuck in the door's lower right quadrant, black with white lettering. A sand-filled bucket, overflowing with cigarette butts, executes the instruction. *What about winter?* you wonder, immediately assuring yourself that you'll never find out.

You fumble all of your items, attempting to hold them in your left hand: your book, your phone, and your pack of cigarettes all stacked together, your lighter precariously wedged under your thumb. Oh, there's your wallet, stuck in the storage sleeve in the door. You hate sitting on it when you drive and always tuck it there, a habit so ingrained it's never remembered. You reach for your wallet and the lighter clatters to the pavement, skipping and rolling straight under the car. Of course.

Fuck.

"Sir?" Sir Jiffy Lube calls from the door. *How many times can you call me "sir," Sir?*

"Be right there!" you call, waving. And there goes the precious pack of cigarettes.

"Jesus fucking Christ," you mutter as you kneel down on the pavement, still holding your book and phone in your left hand. *Dangling on the cross*, you finish in your head, remembering the favorite shock-quality phrase of someone you used to wait tables with. He uttered it whenever the opportunity arose, and now, apparently, so do you. Internally, at least.

Daintily unwilling to lower yourself all the way to the pavement, you blindly reach under the car with your free hand, groping, succeeding only in pushing the lighter further away.

"Fucking *cooperate*," speaking directly to the inanimate object now, realizing that you've done so aloud only as you do.

Dumping dainty, now belly flat on the ground and finally seeing all the way under the car, you reach for and retrieve your lighter. You stand as nonchalantly as possible, brushing pavement dust off your jeans, nearly overwhelmed by the urge to yell, "Got it!," thankfully restraining yourself, just as you restrain yourself from jogging to catch up with Sir Jiffy Lube at the door.

"Sorry about that," you say, chuckling with, you hope, just the right amount of chagrin, attempting your own artificial energy as you join him, more than a little ashamed that you feel the need to do so.

"No problem, *sir!*" he booms, his tone shaming yours. *How does he maintain that all day?*

Quieting slightly, he continues, "Okay, sir, so coffee's in that corner, TV's on that wall, sit wherever you like, we'll be with you in a Jiffy." Was that really a capital J you heard? *Brilliantly consistent marketing*, you think, or perhaps, *consistently brilliant marketing*, following his gesturing arm around the room, observing that all but a couple of chairs are occupied by waiting customers, most of them staring blankly at the television mounted high on that wall, their heads uniformly tilted up. None appear to be drinking the coffee because, you imagine, the room smells like any coffee brewing that occurred here did so a very long time ago. Or perhaps it's just that oil smells like scorched coffee. Didn't someone used to say to imagine coffee when you smell a skunk?

One customer has a leashed dog, a smallish mutt that looks like an underfed German shepherd crossed with a beagle. A shaft of that particular pink lazily dangles between the dog's back legs, obscenely large in relation to his body, proudly announcing his sex. *Lipstick,* you remember someone's reference to a dog's dick. *Would that you could be so confident, Dominic,* you can't help the thought.

The dog's owner, a middle-aged woman wearing a flowing orange dress reminiscent of Tibetan monks and mascara that reminds you, approvingly, of Joy Division, has placed her purse on the chair next to hers, perhaps holding the seat for someone, perhaps simply staking out a degree of separation from the man sitting two chairs to her left, the only person in the room who appears to want conversation. He meets your eyes and smiles hopefully. *Love will tear us apart,* you think, and quickly look away.

The only other vacant seat is occupied by a water bottle, ostensibly the property of the woman sitting next to it. She studiously ignores your approach, apparently engrossed in the auto parts commercial broadcasting from the television.

"Excuse me, is this seat taken?" you ask. She glances at you, annoyed. You gesture to the chair and notice that water has dripped on it, creating a half-dollar sized puddle in the lowest part of the plastic bucket seat.

"Oh. Sorry," she says, reluctantly removing her water bottle to her lap. Observing no option that wouldn't create conflict, you sit directly in the small puddle, hoping your jeans will absorb it without transferring the moisture directly to the skin of your ass, consciously keeping your long legs from encroaching on your new neighbor's space, directing them toward the door—the OPEN door—instead.

As soon as you've settled yourself, you realize that you left your pack of cigarettes lying where it fell in the parking lot. *Seriously?*

You can see the black package from where you sit, just waiting to be run over and crushed. You briefly consider the embarrassment of vacating your seat so soon after the rigmarole of claiming it, particularly wondering what your already annoyed neighbor will think of you but quickly decide that you cannot accept the loss of your cigarettes. The pack is nearly full, worth a quarter of what this oil change will cost, and most important, you'll want one as soon as you're free of this place if not sooner. Suddenly the little water puddle you sat in soaks all the way through your pants, and you realize that you now have a wet spot on your ass.

As you prepare to rise, wet spot and all, you notice Sir Jiffy Lube emerging from the garage to retrieve your car. You observe as he sees your cigarettes and, with barely any pause, scoops them up, turns on his heel, and jogs toward the OPEN door. Leaning just inside, he raises your pack above his head and yells at you from less than four feet away, "Sir, are these *your* cigarettes?"

"Yes," you whisper, holding out your hand. *Like Oliver Twist.*

"No problem, sir. If you intend to smoke, we ask that you stand on the other side of the lot. So as not to disturb the other customers. Butts go here," pointing to the overflowing bucket at his feet.

"Thank you," you say, barely audible, any plans of smoking while you wait thoroughly dashed. As he hands over your pack, your phone, which has been resting on your thigh, clatters to the floor. You pick it up and stand just long enough to secure your phone in your right pocket, your cigarettes in your left. You take this opportunity to surreptitiously pass a hand over your ass, attempting, unsuccessfully, to assess the water damage, and quickly sit back down, clutching your book.

Your neighbor leans to her right, away from you, clarifying her dissociation from the source of so much unwanted commotion. You're reminded of that scene in *The DaVinci Code*, Tom Cruise's explanation of Jesus and Mary leaning away from each other in *The Last Supper*, forming a V between them—the chalice.

No, idiot, that was Tom Hanks. Tom Cruise doesn't know shit about the Holy

Grail. You nearly laugh aloud. *What an excellent conversation starter*, you think, immediately choosing not to follow through on the thought.

Instead you open your book, attempting to push the television's drone to the background. Paul Auster's *The Invention of Solitude*. Ever since discovering his more recent *Winter Journal*, you gobble up Auster's nebulous thoughts, expressed in such beautiful prose, at every opportunity. Including, it seems, in the waiting room at Jiffy Lube.

How very Austerly of you, you think as you read about his time spent living and writing in a shoddy rented room in some decrepit Manhattan structure poised above the Holland Tunnel, a cigar smoke–soaked building shared with working-class, self-employed individuals who, unlike Auster, don't actually live there. Electricians and plumbers and a pair of Italian brothers who manufacture plastic display letters for marquees and are the primary source of all that cigar smoke. And among them, this literary titan-to-be, living cheap while separated from his wife and writing about the ever-complicated nature of the father-son relationship.

While his wife and child continued residing in their recently shared home in upstate Duchess County, Auster relocated to this unfriendly writing environment in anticipation of their divorce. Perhaps this decision was entirely financial, but you tend to think that he was, to some degree at least, punishing himself.

In the tangential manner of such associations, a memory of a little town along Route 22, about two hours north of the City, very near your own early childhood home in Duchess County, suddenly invades your thoughts: Austerlitz, right smack in the middle of the area your mother still calls "the UFO corridor," always insisting that the two of you witnessed more than one such phenomenon when you lived there as a child. As you think these thoughts, distracted from the open book in your lap, your gaze settles on a young man across the waiting room. He appears to be attempting the look of pop-punk skateboarders circa 1994.

Twenty-two years later, that year remains etched in your memory, perhaps the worst of many bad childhood years, the year that all the anxieties of your youth pressed into a sharp, stabbing blade, steel folded into a handmade chef's knife crafted just for you, its point constantly pressed against your back, prodding you forward while biting your spine, drawing blood no matter how you moved. The young man's wallet is connected to his baggy jeans by a chain, his limp Mohawk is a little half-assed, his dark blue Dickies work shirt and bright red Puma sneakers a little too new. His eyes are glued to the television like everyone else.

You think, *Austerlitz, brah. Austerlitz.* Just as your more privileged high school peers, many of whom embodied the very look this young man is trying to replicate, reverently referred to their weekend snowboarding adventures at Stowe: *Stowe, brah. Stowe.* That romanticized town of your youth, unimaginably far away, embodying the culture of wealth you encountered every day but were never allowed to participate in. Now that town is less than an hour's drive from where you sit, forcing yourself not to squirm against your sodden pants while tending to the most banal possible necessity: an oil change.

Back then, those knowing snowboarders seemed to effortlessly rhyme *Stowe* with *brah*, speaking their own private language you still find yourself imitating, helpless to escape the envy of your youth. It occurs to you that the maddening, neurotic anxiety that creeps over you in this sort of situation as you near middle age is very much akin to the constant feeling of near panic that ruled you back then, in those dark teenage years, when the boy you were spent an embarrassing amount of time trying, failing, to be one of those brahs. Just as you tried—and failed—to escape what happened to you.

A nudge at your leg distracts you from your thoughts. Looking down, you discover Tibetan Joy Division lady's skinny little dog nosing at you, tongue lolling, smiling an infectious dog smile. His mistress, engrossed in the television, has dropped his leash.

Although this dog looks nothing like her, his behavior reminds you of your childhood black Lab, Skye, your most constant companion on the streets of Litchfield in your youth. Your version of Oblio's Arrow, your partner in banishment, your best excuse to avoid home and the fear that awaited you there. Your best excuse to avoid your stepfather.

"Hi, buddy," you quietly greet the dog, smiling to yourself as you fold your book over your thumb and offer your other hand to his nose. What made him choose you? Did he smell your anxiety?

Answering your thought, the dog immediately tilts his blocky head, pressing it into your open palm. He inches closer, stepping on your feet with his front paws, angling to get between your legs, closer still, his tail manically wagging, his smile widening.

Perhaps he wants to help.

Imagine your daily routine, your comforts, your anxieties, the everyday stresses of your life, the lengths you go to trying to mitigate them.

Imagine where you live, the spaces you regularly navigate. Where do you feel safe?

Imagine your home.

Now inhabit mine.

HOME: MAY 2016

I AM HOME AGAIN, but this has never been my home. When I was a boy and he was still married to my mother, my stepfather used to admonish, "Stop acting like a guest in your own house," despising my need to go unnoticed, to never demand anything, to make myself small; ignoring that he had fostered that need since I was ten years old, when he began violating me. And earlier still, from my first memories of him, all those years he spent grooming me, preparing for the rape to come.

I am home again, but while decades have passed and I've long since made my own life with a woman who knows all my secrets and still decides to stay, a life in which I'm able to make demands and have them met, a life full of love and joy and mostly without fear, there's no room for that life here. Twenty-six years have passed since he last laid his hands on me, and although he no longer lives here, this will always be my stepfather's home.

I am home again, but here I am still a guest.

CLIMATE CHANGE

SUMMER HAS COME early to Litchfield. April only just ended, and the afternoons are already reaching eighty degrees.

My mother joins me outside, sinking her short, overweight frame into a deeply cushioned faux wicker chair on the stone patio behind the house. She emits a series of tired, defeated sighs between sips of her ubiquitous "frothy coffee," a homemade, oversized cappuccino that she consumes four times daily; three in the morning before heading off to work, one in the afternoon after returning home. This is her fourth. She sets her mug aside, tucking her shoulder-length grey hair behind her ears, exposing her dark-circled eyes, smiling uncertainly.

"What will I do once the house is sold?" she asks without preamble. With barely a breath, she continues: "Where will I live? What if I don't get enough money from the sale to buy another house? Will I be able to get a mortgage? Are you sure I should quit teaching? Maybe I should stay another year. I really wish you'd quit smoking, baby."

Ignoring her last comment with the patience I've been trying to apply to those oft-repeated larger questions, I take a lengthy drag on my cigarette, careful to exhale away from her face. The smoke curls back in her direction despite my effort.

"You'll be fine, Mom," I say, trying to keep my voice positive and engaged. I must check the monotone that will bely my weariness with her constant questions, her constant need for assurance. "You'll live with us in Vermont for as long as you need. And no, you shouldn't stay at your job for another year. It doesn't make sense. They don't pay you enough. You'll just be working to make a high rent payment on some house you don't even like that's five hours away from all your kids. Besides, you can collect Social Security, and you're going to do just fine from the sale of the house."

I sip my beer and watch her eyes. There it is, the unspoken judgment, following the bottle on its way to my mouth. It's three o'clock in the afternoon. I've been working on the house since she left for school at seven this morning. I've spent my day in the basement, a sodden sub-terranean pit that's been ignored for years. It's been a herculean job that started with mold remediation just a few days ago and will con-clude with hiding the ancient asbestos tiles under a new floor that I in-tend to finish by the end of the week. Once the basement is done, only a few painting projects and cleaning will remain. The realtor will put the house on the market in two weeks, my final deadline. I'm exhausted. To hell with whatever my mother thinks about my drinking habits.

"If we ever get it on the market," she laughs lightly, nervously, turn-ing away, waving smoke from her face. "What do you want for dinner, baby? Pizza?"

We agree to eat pizza in front of the television. We'll watch *Game of Thrones*. We'll sit on the love seat in the little den upstairs, my sis-ter's childhood bedroom, elbow to elbow. A thirty-eight-year-old man made boy again by the ghosts in this house, exclaiming at the violence of someone else's imagined world. And for a little while, at least, there will be no more questions, no more assurances.

FIRST VIOLIN

THE ATTIC IS DARK *and full of terrors*, I think as I finally tackle the job I've been putting off throughout the three months I've spent preparing the house for sale. Litchfield has only gotten hotter as May turns to June, and it must be well over a hundred degrees in the attic. Sweat immediately pops out on my face and begins to pour down, stinging my eyes behind their contact lenses. I silently berate myself for procrastinating over this chore for so long. I should have done it three months ago, when I first arrived, while the cold lingered. Now there's no more putting it off. Still, I can't quite make myself move from my seated position, perched on the edge of the access hole, my legs dangling above the ladder and the hallway beneath.

Directly to my left, the brick chimney stack is crumbling, evidence of a leak in the rooftop flashing, never fixed. All around me, black garbage bags lay among the exposed floor joists, filled with clothes unceremoniously tossed up through the hole at various points over the last three decades. A rolled up rug that must be twelve feet long lies along the joists to my right, tucked up under the eaves. I briefly wonder how anyone got it up here and immediately decide that here it will stay, closing be damned.

I can't move from my perch until some room is made, so I begin tossing the bags of clothes down to my wife, who is waiting in the hallway below my swinging feet. The brittle black plastic is hot to the touch and emits a mist of white mold as it's disturbed for the first time in who knows how long. I breathe shallowly through my mouth. A bag bursts apart as it hits the floor below, directly in front of my wife's feet. Men's

clothes, covered in mildew, reeking of hot dampness. Khakis and cor-
duroys, blazers and button downs, all from a different decade, all his.

"Fuck!" my wife exclaims from below, wrinkling her nose and waving away the poisonous cloud.

"You okay?" I call from my perch above, prepared to scramble down
the ladder.

"I'm fine," she says, disgusted but already gathering up my rapist's
clothes in a new, clear garbage bag.

"You're sure?" I ask for good measure, ashamed that I would take any
excuse to continue procrastinating.

"Yes," she reassures me, head down, working without hesitation
among the decrepit clothes. I experience an intense rush of gratitude
for my beautiful, elegant wife, her tall frame bent double, her face hidden by her long loose ponytail as her long delicate hands labor at the
most inelegant sort of work. Would anyone else be willing to do this
with me? Certainly not my sisters, who have remained conspicuously
absent from the actual work of helping our mother move on from her
former life with their father. My wife looks up at me and smiles rue-
fully, stretching, resituating her hair in a new, tighter ponytail. "I'm
fine."

"Okay. I'm going in."

Dark and full of terrors, I think again as I finally make my way into
the attic's depths. And it is. Any flashlights that might have been in
the house are already packed. My only light comes from my iPhone
propped against the chimney stack. It illuminates an alarming collection of wasp's nests built against the inside slats of vents at either end
of the attic. They look old and dry, but I hear buzzing. I move quickly,
crouched, trying to avoid barking my spine against the rafters, failing
often.

In the far corner, past boxes of old books I'd hoped would be worth
salvaging but that crumble under my touch, back under the eaves opposite the long snake of rug that is staying up here forever, I discover
my grandfather's violins. The thought that they might be hopelessly
warped from the heat, that mold might be eating those storied old

instruments in their cases as surely as it was eating my stepfather's old clothes blends with my stinging eyes and my aching back and my mother's constant questions and my wife's having just been forced to handle my rapist's discarded wardrobe, clothes he likely wore during the darkest era of my life, and goes Gozer, white hot rage bursting from my sweating pores.

How could they leave these up here?

These are my mother's father's instruments, tools of my long-dead grandfather's art and trade as first violinist of the White House Orchestra, the soft-spoken, kind man who made his living playing music for presidents, the man who adopted my mother and loved me, his only grandson, unconditionally. I don't share his blood any more than I share my stepfather's, but I did share Oreo cookies and ice cream with him as a toddler, despite his already being half-blinded by diabetes.

This was the man who, so unlike my stepfather, never boasted about his talent despite the inheritance he left my mother, money later squandered by the family I was never allowed to participate in, having been paid out by the US Marine Corps, a tangible recognition of the decades my grandfather spent entertaining the leadership of America and visiting heads of state, all of whom enjoyed the music he produced on these very violins. And here they are, discarded among the crumbling books and moldy clothes.

Recently, I decided to take my grandfather's name.

BROKEN WINDOWS

EVERY ROOM IN THIS house contains at least one broken window. Most are mildly cracked, some severely damaged. I spent the afternoon inspecting them, deciding which will need to be replaced or repaired before the house goes on the market.

Now, standing in the dark kitchen at midnight, trying to close the window above the sink, I realize that I missed this one. I wonder whether it's worth fixing any of them. Leaving the window ajar, I fumble for a water glass, opening the refrigerator for light.

"I gave you my name!" my stepfather often stormed at me in this kitchen, long after the rest of the family retreated to their beds, thin walls providing a flimsy illusion of insulation from this familiar exchange. "When I found you, you were a bastard, you were living in shit. Literal shit!"

I stand in the same place I stood then, by the refrigerator, holding its door open, staring at the butcher block surface of the kitchen island where he so often propped his elbows, leaning toward me, his broad, jowly face contorted and red. He always struggled with his weight back then, often swinging fifty pounds in a matter of months. As a teenager, I learned to become particularly attuned to his mood when he was on the heavy end of such a swing. His potential for anger seemed directly proportionate to his girth. Remembering those long, dark years, my eyes fix on two old stains in the wood, made obvious in the dim light, my imagination insisting that they mark the spots where his elbows dug in, supporting his weight as he raged.

I pour a glass of water to take to bed in what used to be my stepfather's bedroom, and his father's bedroom before. My mother, concerned that mold spores from the basement were making her ill, no longer sleeps in the house proper. She moved across the breezeway to the small suite where her mother-in-law lived her final years; Grandma, the once Tough Cookie who never failed to arrange livery service to the train station so I could visit my father, back in the days when my stepfather used to call me a bastard.

Recently, my mother explained that our dog at the time, a rambunctious Sheltie she ultimately rehomed before the man who would become my stepfather moved in, back when everything was about to change in that little cottage we shared on campus at the school in Duchess County, once shat on the floor in my bedroom. Unfortunately, the dog's excrement went unnoticed until their date that evening, when my future stepfather came for dinner. I often wonder what that man was doing in my bedroom, back in those early days, before he replaced my father's name with his own.

Ultimately, I decided to replace both of my fathers' surnames with my mother's maiden name. But that was my own decision, a show of solidarity in support of my mother when she finally divorced my rapist.

I was never a bastard.

HOME: JUNE 2016

I AM HOME AGAIN, but the fact that I am now the man of this house is not justice. When he was still married to my mother, my stepfather used to beg, "Please, Dominic, I just want to be close to you. I want you to trust me. Why won't you trust me? I'm your father. I raised you from nothing," disallowing argument, disallowing the truth. Disallowing me.

I am home again, but no matter how empowering it feels to finally claim agency in this house after years and years of none, I am consumed by the silent, crushing anxiety that perpetually ruled me here. All of my necessary lies rush back, the stress of their repetition evident in every corner. There is the chair I sank into while he peppered me with questions and demands, there is the bathroom where I pretended to shit for hours, there is the window I escaped through at night.

I am home again, but here, I am still a child.

DOUBLE HELIX

MOWING THE LAWN was a chore exclusively mine as a boy. Back then, I timed the mowing to coincide with my stepfather's presence; a better excuse for avoiding him at home than sitting on the toilet for unreasonably prolonged periods. Back then, I mowed in slow circles from the outside in, allowing the mower's blades to catch only a few inches of uncut grass on each subsequent pass, delaying completion for as long as possible, an hour or more. I created excuses to further extend the simple chore, teaching myself how to change the mower's oil, unnecessarily doing so before every mowing, stopping every fifteen minutes to fastidiously clean the blades with WD-40. Thinking all the while, *Where is he? What is he doing? Will he leave? Is he watching? Waiting?* Until finally I ran out of excuses. The pattern created near the end was clearly a J, his first initial. I dreaded the end, the conclusion of my excuse to be otherwise occupied. I took intense pleasure in slowly whittling his initial away to nothing.

Two decades later I find myself using the same mower, a perfectly preserved antique thanks to those years of constant, unnecessary maintenance. Now I mow the lawn differently. Quickly, diagonally, in twenty-inch strips back and forth, cutting the grass forward, then back, creating a uniform pattern. A golf course writ small. Now I take pleasure in the simplicity of the manual labor, enjoying its physicality and the Zen quality of the relatively mindless, repetitive work, briefly freeing me from the perpetual anxieties of home. Start to finish, it now takes thirty minutes.

It's Wednesday. Connecticut is always significantly warmer than my home in Vermont, but this year's El Niño has driven already rising temperatures well beyond the norm for June in Litchfield, regularly cresting ninety degrees as July approaches. And it's humid. As I begin to sweat, I find myself looking forward to the reward of a cold, guiltless beer. Thirty minutes.

Despite my newfound pleasure in mowing the lawn, I still find myself occasionally using it as an avoidance tactic. The impetus to do so now certainly doesn't carry the imperative it did then. Now it's rooted in a new, unanticipated relationship.

Although my stepfather is, in fact, no longer my stepfather, his brother remains my uncle. Despite his peripheral involvement in my childhood, these days my uncle asserts more than an uncle's usual role, playing at doting suitor to my mother and concerned father to me in the aftermath of her divorce. An alum of the school where I grew up a faculty brat, my uncle has recently taken a position in their administration, helping to grow the school's already outsized endowment and assisting with the admission of new students, expertise he's employed at other prep schools over the course of his long career. Now I can't help but wonder, does my uncle understand that his very purpose, the apex of that long career, stymies my own justice?

At my wedding last year, my uncle earnestly told me, "I just want you to know that not all the men in my family are monsters." Now that his work has brought him closer to home, my uncle makes it his habit to take my mother to dinner every Wednesday, a kindness I appreciate even as I dread his presence. Like my mother, my uncle is full of questions.

Just as I'm beginning to lose myself in my work, my uncle pulls into the driveway in his newly leased SUV, leaning out of his open window as he parks.

"Ah, do you have to mow right now?" he calls from his car. I intended to be in the backyard by the time he arrived, where I could avoid him altogether. Unfortunately, my mother delayed me with her daily litany of questions, always the same: *What will I do? Where will I live?* And, unspoken but underlying them all: *Who will take care of me?* I pretend not to hear my uncle as I let the mower sputter to a stop, forcing a smile as he climbs out, waving me down.

I steel myself for the tiresome, well-meant advice he is wont to offer on everything from what to paint, what to fix, what to keep, and what to discard, to what to skip working on altogether.

My uncle no longer speaks to my stepfather, a decision he arrived at after a couple of years spent unsuccessfully attempting to convince his brother to seek help and try to atone for what he did to me. I am deeply grateful for my uncle's tacit acknowledgment of what I survived. Perhaps his acknowledgment will be catching.

But I wonder again, as I so often have, how my uncle would react if he knew that I hold the school where he earned his high school diploma, the school he continues to promote, very nearly as culpable as my stepfather. Would he champion me—or the school, his alma mater, now his employer? Would he seek justice—or self-preservation?

My uncle's appearance differs from his brother in every possible way. Once a marathon runner, my uncle remains relatively trim even, or perhaps especially, as he approaches seventy. His tailored suit, tight Windsor knot, and spotless new SUV are a sharp juxtaposition to my stepfather's preference for worn khakis, tweeds, and his battered ten-year-old Subaru.

My uncle's voice and affect, however, are remarkably reminiscent. He exudes the same sense of privilege that my stepfather always did, bestowed on them with their father's Social Register name—the name that was also mine until I forsook it at sixteen, when I escaped. He speaks in circles, like my stepfather, and while his words are unfailingly encouraging and complimentary—so unlike my stepfather's— they barely conceal subtle criticisms under a blanket of condescension so natural to him that I could never possibly offer contradiction. To do so would be as futile as disciplining an infant for selfishness.

"Ah, must you do it now?" he calls again as I cross the lawn. "How's the basement coming? Did you replace that door yet? No? Oh dear. Oh well, soon. Can't you take a break, join us for dinner? How long does it take? What, about an hour? Ah, what a job. And in this heat? Surely you can do it later? Tomorrow? Have dinner with us, won't you? Gotta get that door done, you know?"

He delivers his sentences in a hearty, slightly-too-loud voice accompanied by a note of disbelief, each statement punctuated with rising inflection, calculated questions so long practiced they are no longer calculated. I remind myself that he only ever means well, and in that thought, I'm reminded of my grandmother, his mother, Grandpa's beloved, the Tough Cookie. After Grandpa's death, her characteristic toughness had abruptly dissipated. In the years leading up to her own death, nearly two decades ago, she perfected the art of indirect requests.

"Would you like more salad, dear?" she'd ask from her place at the dinner table to my left. I'd notice that the salad bowl was actually on my right, out of her reach, and realize the expected response, "No, thank you, Grandma, but would you?" She would protest as I served her, then promptly clean her plate.

I reflect that manipulation takes many forms. I wonder, is it possible that particular types are inherited? Bred in families as surely as eye color?

"I'd love to," I assure my uncle as I embrace his stooped back and feel his arthritic hands drawing me close, "But it could rain any time now, and it's supposed to keep raining through tomorrow." I take his shoulders in my hands and step back. "Why don't you two go out without me and bring home some leftovers? That'll give me time to finish up and jump in the shower, then we can all have some wine and chat."

"Ah, you're a good boy," he says, clapping my back once more as he disengages. "Don't work too hard," he turns away and calls my mother.

"Sissay!" he yells toward the house, totally unaware of how deeply that particular address—delivered in a tone so close to my stepfather's—turns my stomach. A geyser of hot acid rushes from my gut to the back of my tongue, my mouth instantly sweating with nausea. I want to spit but resist, forcing myself to swallow instead.

My uncle disappears into the house, searching for my mother, thankfully more interested in her than me. I wonder whether, to some degree at least, he shares my desire for avoidance. I gratefully start the mower again, eager to finish quickly so I can enjoy a beer and a few cigarettes in solitude before they return.

ASBESTOS

THE HOUSE IS A 1950s-era center-staired Cape of some 1,800 square feet that sits on half an acre, about half a mile west of the town green. The neighborhood is solidly upper middle class, a street of similarly tidy white houses connecting the public grade school to the prerevolutionary mansions that dominate the avenues to the east. My stepfather's parents purchased the house in the late eighties, downsizing, if that term even existed back then, from their previous home, the huge, rambling 1745 colonial built on that beautifully hedged corner lot in Bridgehampton, very like those nearby mansions, but a short bike ride from the open Atlantic Ocean.

Unfortunately, the Hampton house became too expensive and difficult to maintain as my grandparents aged. And they wanted to be closer to their grandchildren. To me. So they sold the old mansion and purchased the little Litchfield Cape in cash, cramming it full of antique heirlooms once housed in twice the space. Unable to hate my grandparents for selling my summers, I hated the new house instead. My grandfather passed away just a couple of years later, and I grew to hate it more.

Weary from years of housing his family in the cramped campus apartment provided along with the teaching salaries he and my mother drew from the nearby prep school, my stepfather jumped at the opportunity. My grandmother was ailing as well, after all, and needed constant care.

After a year spent arguing with his brother, my stepfather finally convinced their mother that the house should be his, mollifying my uncle by relinquishing most of the antiques and family oil portraits to his care. My stepfather mortgaged the house and arranged contractors as soon as they struck their deal, remodeling the garage into a small in-law suite, downsizing his mother once again as he took the bedroom where his father died. My little half sisters were each given one of the remaining two upstairs bedrooms.

I was put in the basement, where I now stand, shocked as I take inventory of the damage, trying to imagine how I ever possibly lived down here. All along the walls, the paneling that hides the concrete foundation is stained like cardboard left out in the rain, awaiting trash day. The baseboard heaters are rusted to dust in places, beyond repair. The asbestos floor tiles are buckled, ruined, emitting carcinogens as they rot. The door to this room, once my bedroom, is flaking at the bottom where it was immersed in standing water. I wonder whether a heavy coat of paint will be sufficient to hide the mold creeping up toward its handle. My mother insisted that I wear a paper mask while working down here. I intended to comply but remove the mask when my breath begins fogging my glasses. I need to see clearly.

Of course, when I was a teenager, this room was finished, clean and warm, even relatively dry, and the two stories that separated it from my stepfather's bedroom provided all the incentive I needed to acclimate to the rumbling boiler and rattling pipes. And there was the window.

Cut high in the wall, the window opens into a shallow well in the backyard. It's just large enough for a properly motivated teenager to slip through. As I often did, escaping into the night, furtively traipsing all over town in all sorts of weather, my fear of discovery trumped by the thrill of stolen freedom.

Back then, I would wait until the boiler finished cycling, marking the end of my stepfather's nightly ablutions. I would patiently count to one thousand, assuring myself that he was well and truly down for the night; if not fully asleep, at least too comfortable in his bed to be bothered by an errant noise. Finally, I would carefully open the window, easing my lanky teenage body, already fully clothed and shoed, from my lofted bed through the opening, outside, pulling my backpack behind.

And then I was off, racing through the moonlit yard, cutting through the woods, angling toward streets that led to the homes of friends and later girlfriends with more welcoming parents, hoping to find companionship for my all-night adventure, content to wander alone if not. I was prepared either way: a mixtape-loaded Walkman provided a soundtrack for my wandering, a book and an Itty Bitty Book Light waited to provide entertainment should I be unlucky in my quest for company. Sometimes I found it, sometimes I didn't, but either way, for a brief time at least, I was free. Safe.

The window has been broken for years. While it was once undoubtedly my saving grace, it's become the root of my current problems. Inspecting the damage, I note my stepfather's half-assed attempt at repair. Layers of once clear, pliant plastic now stiff and opaque with age, hurriedly taped over the gaping frame; shards of glass left where they fell who knows how long ago. The plastic and tape are so degraded that they appear to be held in place only by their weathered rigidity. I carefully remove the glass from the deep sill piece by piece, dropping the shards into a cardboard box at my feet.

Once the area is safe, I begin gingerly pulling at the plastic, steeling myself for what might lie behind. All at once the plastic breaks away, followed by a cascade of foul water, drenching me, my cardboard box, and the broken asbestos tiles beneath my feet.

TWIST

"LISTEN, BABY, WILL YOU please talk to your sister? I'm really going to need all my children after this is over, and I'm worried about you two, you know? You haven't spoken in a long time. I'm sure all you need is one good talk. This has all just been so hard, you know? I just want nice Sunday dinners in Vermont. All my kids around the table with me, laughing like we used to. I just don't want it to be awkward, and the longer we let this lie, the harder it's going to get, do you know what I'm saying? I just love you so much, and I want everything to be okay. Everything's going to be okay, right?"

My mother stands at the top of the basement stairs, nervously twitching her right leg in her usual rhythm. She was adopted just late enough in life to miss that period of infant-parent touch so imperative to development, and it shows. She rocks constantly, whether cooking dinner, painting, talking on the phone, or sitting in an overstuffed chair in the living room with her frothy coffee. When particularly nervous or caffeinated, her rocking becomes something akin to the twist, her ankle swiveling out from the ball of her foot at least twice each second, her leg following suit, her upper body bouncing along in time. How I despise this dance, the sadness it brings.

"Yes, Mom," I answer, rising from my work burying all that broken asbestos under new, cheap, cream-colored linoleum, grateful for the excuse to stretch, annoyed by the interruption.

I'm nearly finished. It no longer hurts to breathe in the basement. The mold is gone, rotted walls removed, fresh sheetrock installed, broken window sealed, and fresh white paint covers all. The basement is now the cleanest part of the house. Or will be, as soon as the new floor is finally down. I grope for my phone, silencing the NPR pundits arguing from its tiny speaker, my soundtrack as I work.

"I'm happy to call her," I say, leaning against the railing at the bottom of the stairs, looking up at her, patience just beyond reach. "But listen, Mom, because I really need you to understand this." Always supposedly the articulate one, now sweaty, cramped, and exhausted, suddenly unable to find my own words, I shock myself by uttering words too close to my stepfather's hated vocabulary: "I can't be the only one to make an overture. I need her to meet me halfway, at least. She really hurt me, you know?"

Disgust turns my stomach as I hear myself parroting my mother's nervous punctuation and blending it into a surreal, hybrid language that includes something akin to my stepfather's circular lexicon of meaningless arguments. I recognize this feeling. I've experienced it countless times before. It's the harbinger of a particular sort of anger, fraught with frustration, always seeking an outlet, a gateway to the side of myself that I've never quite been able to articulate, let alone control. It is, for lack of another word, madness.

As a boy always seeking to name the unnameable, I called this side of myself Gozer. The ultimate villain of *Ghostbusters*: Gozer the Destructor, Gozer the Gozerian. A silly name chosen by a young teenager, utterly ridiculous, really, but still somehow right. Gozer the Destructor is always right. Just as he is always, unfailingly, destructive.

Intellectually, I'm aware that Gozer and his uncontrollable rage is meant to be directed strictly at my stepfather, my ultimate villain. I had hoped that I'd dispelled Gozer six years ago, when I finally exposed my stepfather, but I was wrong.

Gozer lingers. And when that feeling threatens, when Gozer lurks near, he leaves no room for intellect. Gozer will attack whoever is handy, no matter how loved.

Now, looking up the stairs at my mother, I put all my effort into control, desperately attempting to keep Gozer's worst in check.

I succeed. Partially.

"I can't take all the responsibility for this, you know?" I say. "I need you to help me, I need you to *show* her. It can't all come from me. She needs to hear it from you too, you know?" I finish lamely, aware that I'm barely making sense, my disgust compounded as, despite my effort to quash Gozer, I see his words taking effect. Just as if my stepfather had uttered them, my mother's ankle swivels faster, faster, her face tightens, she is near tears and it's all my fault.

"Okay, baby," my mother says, her voice so small. "Good. Are you ready for a break? Want a frothy coffee?"

"I just want to finish," I say, turning away from her, allowing Gozer to silently rage within the confines of my thoughts, my hatred for this house turned inward.

HOME: JULY 2016

I AM HOME AGAIN, but while I strive to find forgiveness for my mother, I am helpless before the rage that stifles me in this house. Six years ago, when I exposed him to my mother, my stepfather said, "I don't know, Dominic. I don't know if I can handle this. I really don't know. I might have to kill myself. I really might," usurping my own suicidal intentions, considered month after month, year after year, while he violated me and long thereafter.

I am home again, but no matter how gratifying it felt to hear my rapist's confession, to force his acknowledgment in front of my weeping mother, I was not grateful. "Shut the fuck up," I said without hesitation, definitively, firmly, intentionally taking my stand against this pathetic little man, considering him clearly that way for the first time. "You fucking coward. I survived you; you can sure as hell survive me."

I am home again, but here I am always angry.

PUBLIC BROADCAST

"OH, BABY, MY DEAREST BOY, how could I let this happen to you?" my mother croaks through tears. Racking sobs match the gyrating twist in her leg even as she sits, constantly in motion, constantly in pain, her face broken wide open. "How could I not know? How did I miss it? You're my baby. You know that you're my favorite, don't you? Always. I love you so, so much. You know that, don't you?"

I stand above my mother as she sinks into the loveseat in the little upstairs den, her grocery store sushi dinner discarded at her side. PBS NewsHour is muted on the television, the elderly anchor silently gesticulating, throwing weird light around the dark room. I focus on my mother, avoiding the distraction as I absorb her words.

My mother loves me more than her daughters. I always knew that, but her confirmation is shocking, a dirty admission never to be voiced. I try to control my response, desperate to steer myself toward something clean, but I can't get beyond a single word. The only match for my emotions, the despised, hollow monosyllable: shame.

"Of course, Mom," I say, woodenly reassuring, kneeling, reaching for her, holding the side of her face in my hand, "I love you. Please don't be sad. Please don't cry. I can't stand to see you cry. I'm fine now. We're fine. I love you so much."

She lunges forward and I take her in my arms, stabilizing her, taking the aftershock of her subsiding sobs. Absorbing her pain even as it compounds my own.

I don't know what else to say. After several moments spent kneeling and rocking, I finally mutter, "I love you, Mom," stroking her hair, willing her to calm. "Everything's okay. I love you."

Nonsense words. Anything to make her stop.
Like soothing an inconsolable child.

GREAT EXPECTATIONS

IT'S TIME. The realtor, so perfectly dressed, so punctual, wearing so much makeup, just finished snapping photos of the house. She arrived exactly two minutes early, just as I wrapped up the painting and my wife completed the cleaning. The casual sexism of our automatically delineated duties disturbed me throughout this incredibly long day. I am painfully aware that I couldn't possibly have done my wife's work in so little time, although she could easily have done mine.

I consider what sort of man I am, generally, as I note my internal criticism of the realtor's appearance, helpless to stop my silent commentary. I wonder whether her astonishingly high designer heels dissuaded her from getting enough exterior photos. The grass is wet, but the property looks best from the bottom of the yard. Are they Manolo Blahniks? I've got to get out of this town, out of this house, back to Vermont. Back to Birkenstocks and Uggs, equally annoying in their own ways, but expected. Familiar. Home.

While my mother painstakingly signs the papers, sitting at the kitchen island where all the important business of this house was ever conducted, I notice that my wife forgot about the pot rack hanging above, invisible in its everyday obviousness. Ancient dust clumps spiral down from the steel hooks and grease-smeared wrought iron. The house is almost certainly the cleanest it's ever been. I appreciate the juxtaposition, a last bit of evidence indicating where we began, perhaps the only remaining marker for how far we've come. *You should've taken "before" photos*, I think, but immediately counter, *for whom?*

I resolve to scrub down the pot rack tomorrow morning, before the realtor's first showing, eliminating the last of the visible filth in this house. This, at least, is a cleaning job that I can do.

In the meantime, I pour a glass of wine and look over my mother's shoulder, trying to restrain myself from rushing her through the paperwork. *You should've bought champagne*, you think, but then, *are we really celebrating?*

Forcing my rambling, exhausted thoughts aside, I smile as the realtor perfunctorily shakes my hand, preparing to leave.

"Thank you," she says. "It looks amazing, better than I hoped for. Really. Amazing! Tomorrow we're live!" She abruptly turns away, abandoning my hand, paperwork tucked neatly under her arm. Her fabulous heels click sharply off the pavement as she strides to her pristine, white SUV. I think of my uncle, how much he'd appreciate her, and experience a wave of overly effusive gratitude of my own.

It must be her professional abruptness: the simple, distinct boundaries of the relationship. She didn't ask too many questions. Or perhaps it's simply that my own job here is nearly over. Something to celebrate, after all.

In the morning, my wife thoroughly cleans the pot rack before I even realize the job is done. I wonder whether I knew she would, wonder whether I've answered my question in its asking. Aren't I supposed to be so enlightened? So sensitive? A truly feminist man?

What separates me from the likes of my stepfather, who always confidently claimed the same? Is it only that I'm not attracted to children, that the thought of sexual contact with a child repulses me? That the thought of hurting a child in any way horrifies me?

Is that enough?

THE GRAPES OF RECESSION

WHAT IS A GREAT *recession if not a depression?* I wonder in response to the NPR commentators in my phone arguing about just how much the economy has improved as I labor. My rented panel truck's silhouette obstructs the view even from the upstairs windows, reminding me of my mother's relative poverty.

Even now, at the end of her long teaching career, about to collect a significant sum from the sale of this house, my mother remains too poor to hire movers. Forty years of uninterrupted work were not enough, her private school teacher's salary barely cresting fifty thousand dollars annually, a sum significantly less than the tuition bill of any of her students. Children with parents named Liam Neeson and Bill Cosby; malleable youths learning about art from my mother alongside the children of lesser-known but equally privileged titans of New York finance. Young people who would grow into adulthood and never have to worry about their fates, in financial terms at least, should their spouses so utterly and completely betray them.

In her divorce from a self-confessed pedophile, a man who openly admitted repeatedly sexually assaulting her son, my mother is still forced to share the burden of his debts, still forced to pay her lawyer who advised her not to pursue alimony as she faces forced retirement and unknown years of old age to follow with no one to support her. When will her great recession end?

These are the questions that brought me back to this house. These are the complications that allow room for my undeniable love for my mother, love that continually elbows its way between all the questions about how she could possibly have ignored — and therefore allowed — what her husband did to me.

While these questions certainly remain and certainly deserve answers, I am also left to wonder: how can I abandon her when the legal establishment has abandoned her, just as it abandoned me? How can I allow the anger I feel toward my mother, no matter how justified, to keep me from helping her when I can? When no one else will? How can I separate the pain of what happened to me from what happened to her?

The difference is clearly identifiable, of course, but what sort of justification is that? Does my pain diminish hers? Can I claim that my pain trumps hers? And even if it does, and it seems clear to me that it does, how can I ignore her, discard her, when I know all too well what it is to be ignored and discarded myself? How can I condone, let alone perpetuate, the same betrayal — my stepfather's betrayal, my mother's betrayal, and that of all those around us, all those who observed even the smallest part of my experience?

The second attic, a small storage space located above the breezeway, is thankfully easier to access than the larger attic where I found my grandfather's violins. An incongruous triangular door built to fit the sloping roofline in the master bedroom provides entry.

My mother calls this door "witchy." She's always hidden it behind a heavy trifold screen nearly as tall as me, and wide, stretching six feet end to end. I've often wondered why she feels the need to so thoroughly obstruct this door. The screen makes the bedroom appear much smaller than it is, a decorating faux pas my mother's strict sense of feng shui normally wouldn't allow.

I set the screen aside, folded, exposing the door. As I pull it open, the heat trapped behind rushes out, a distinct punch of air that conjures an image of ghosts, clamoring to escape. Perhaps the door really is witchy. Perhaps the screen provides a necessary barrier.

The space behind the witchy door is packed to the rafters with years of memories. Stacked boxes overflow with children's clothes and toys, report cards and books. There is my sisters' battered dollhouse; there is the untouched Nordic machine my stepfather bought on one of his exercise whims; there is a trunk I remember from my grandparents' era, the only easily reachable thing in here.

Opening the trunk, I discover a dead mouse atop a stack of folded blankets. The blankets are that particular woven fabric, impossibly soft, powder blues and pastel greens with silky trim, my grandmother's favorites, and mine. As I reach out to touch one, smiling, the mouse moves. Not dead after all, just still, patiently waiting for me to leave, secure in the knowledge that this is its space, not mine. I am the intruder here.

The mouse is right. After spending several moments immobilized, staring at the Tetris stacks, nearly overwhelmed by despair, wondering where to start, I finally drag a few boxes from the top out to the bedroom floor. Consolidating their contents into plastic storage bins, I begin to wonder whether I'll find any evidence of my own childhood among these memories. There are book reports and art projects tracing each of my sisters' lives back to first grade, yearbooks from every year they spent in high school, even my stepfather's blue exam books from NYU. Nothing in this mess indicates that I ever lived here. My presence in this house has effectively been erased. In this house, I was never more than a guest. Just as my stepfather always promised.

Taking a break to mop sweat from my face, stretch, and guzzle water, I turn a complete circle in the bedroom. My gaze settles on the spot where my grandfather died. I consider the three generations of fathers, sons, stepsons, and wives who slept in this room, adjacent to all these boxed up memories.

Although I haven't exactly done much sleeping here. Months of accumulated restless nights spent in this room contributed, at least in part, to my current exhaustion. I tend to rotate through excuses for my insomnia, blaming everything from the stress of dealing with contractors and realtors to the aches and pains of my recent labor. Anything to avoid the ghosts in this room.

Perhaps I understand the need to call depression a great recession after all.

REAL ESTATE

"I HAVE IN MY hand a full-price offer!" The realtor's voice booms from my phone, making me cringe as I strain to hear. Barely twenty-four hours have passed since she snapped her photos and collected the signed papers. "Congratulations!" I immediately wonder whether the price was set high enough. In the next instant, that sense of effusive gratitude I felt for her returns.

"That's wonderful news," I say. "Amazing! Thank you so much."

"No problem," she says, and I can't prevent a touch of Gozer seeping through, whispering from the back of my mind. *Sure, no problem for you, lady. You just made, what, about twelve grand for twenty-four hours' work? You didn't spend three months slaving away in the place. For nothing.*

But Gozer is unkind. After all, the realtor discounted her fee. And she probably put in more like forty hours. And she is the bearer of excellent news, and for that, at least, I am grateful. We exchange another round of congratulations and thank-yous before I rejoin my wife at the table inside.

"We did it," I tell her, trying to keep my voice down, conscious of nearby diners in the restaurant we escaped to while the realtor showed the house. "Full-price offer. We fucking did it."

"Seriously?" my wife asks, her clear, blue eyes shining. "It's over? We can finally get the hell out of here? We can go home?"

"Yes," I answer, suddenly near tears myself. "Finally. Home."

MOTHER'S MYTHOLOGY

"SO LISTEN, BABY, I really need you to tell me that your childhood was okay, that there was at least some happiness there," my mother says over the phone, her voice artificially high, trying for levity.

Two weeks have passed since the realtor sold the house. I'm finally home, in Vermont, settling into our summer rental in the Mad River Valley, enjoying days spent alone with my wife; reading, writing, and walking punctuated by evenings spent grilling and sipping wine on the house's wonderfully private deck. Recovering from the last three months of chores and questions and assurances. We'll return to Connecticut for the final move in just a few short weeks, just before the closing, after which my mother will join us here, in our new home, ending our privacy. But for now, my wife and I bask in the simplicity of these relaxing, rejuvenating summer days.

Until this moment. My mother's words explode in my mind. That madness, always near but carefully controlled, rushes in, momentarily overwhelming my typically even, carefully considered thoughts. Fury takes me, sweeping away my control. All at once, I become that overwrought maniac, that other self that is also mine, usually suppressed but never completely banished: Gozer, the dark side of myself, the thoughtless maniac that I both fear and revel in.

This time, Gozer will not be tempered. I barely keep him from screaming aloud.

Gozer thinks: *What the fuck? What the FUCK? Are you kidding me?*

Gozer wants to shout: *How could you ask me that? How, you crazy fucking bitch, what are you, blind?*

It lasts only a moment, then he is gone, or at least momentarily sequestered again. The Destructor is still near—I've finally accepted that Gozer will always be near—but my next thought is my own.

Oh, Mom, you poor, sad, broken woman.

Sweat beads on my forehead and above my quivering lip as I answer, "Of course, Mom. Of course there was happiness in my childhood. And I owe those happy moments to you. I love you so much."

I say it small, barely able to keep from choking on my words. Barely keeping Gozer the Destructor's screaming profanity in check. I make up some excuse, hang up abruptly, unwilling to risk his return in my mother's presence.

A late night follows, hours spent replaying this conversation and all its implications with my wife over too much wine and too many cigarettes, allowing Gozer to shout himself out.

I spend the following day recovering, sleeping in, and then leisurely setting up our new home. Even Vermont's high mountain valleys are unseasonably warm this summer, and we find it necessary to install an air conditioner in our bedroom.

As I work, I consider how I might blend the abrasive truth of Gozer's madness with my own considerations, searching for balance between the ugly reality and the love I feel for my mother. How can I tell the truth while protecting her from it? Does that balance exist? Can it be found somewhere between Gozer's belligerent profanity and my overly careful, overly considered assurances?

Perhaps this is my own manipulation, a new mutation, a genetic anomaly rooted in the broken family I came from. I can see the words forming in my mind, but will I ever be able to speak them aloud?

I think: *My childhood was awful, Mom, and that only because there's no word to describe what it actually was. I feel lucky to have survived it.*

I think: *I couldn't hope for happiness, Mom. I could only strive for survival. And I did that. I survived.*

I think: *And isn't it wonderful, amazing, really, that you and I can have the relationship we have now? Any sort of relationship at all?*

I think: *Because the truth is, you should have done something. Even if you didn't know everything, you knew enough. Of that, there is no doubt. You should have protected me. And you didn't. You did not.*

And now, here I am, making it okay for you. Protecting you.

As I pull up the sash and prepare to place the air conditioner, I realize that this window in our new house has a crack in it. This home is strictly temporary, and the responsibility to fix it clearly belongs to someone else.

But there's no denying that it's broken.

Acknowledgments

I'm grateful to Susan Steinberg and all those at the University of Iowa Press who believed in this admittedly difficult book and helped bring it to the world, especially Carolyn Brown, Trudi Gershenov, Stephanie Karp, Jim McCoy, Susan Hill Newton, and Meredith Stabel. I'm also grateful to the editors of *Talking Soup*, who published an early version of "Distilled" under the title "Sour Mash," and to the editors of *Memory-house Magazine*, who published an equally early version of "Coffee Talk" under the title "The Pot."

The boundaries of memoir are naturally limited to a subjective account of a particular span of time. I am continually, wonderfully astonished by my mother, Cecilia Bucca, and my sisters, Christina Timrud and Sarah Keller, who have grown and changed alongside my own growth and change, throughout the writing of this book and well beyond the action it describes. To acknowledge that these changes haven't been easy feels horribly inadequate, so let me simply say: I'm deeply grateful for your love and support, and for the new family we've created together from the wreckage that was.

I also owe an unpayable debt of gratitude, albeit in absentia, to my father and stepmother, Bill and Jaye Miller, at whose kitchen table I learned a new way of life and, much later, hesitantly began writing what would ultimately become this book. Thank you for believing in me. You are both sorely missed.

Additionally, this project would not have been possible without the following:

Muriel Shockley, who helped me see the beginning and stayed through the end; most devoted mentor, constant reader, sometimes therapist, once or twice a colleague, and always dear friend. And excellent wining and dining companion.

My teachers, recent and past, especially Connie May Fowler, Rigoberto Gonzalez, Barbara Hurd, and Sue William Silverman at Vermont College of Fine Arts, as well as Bill Bucklin, Jocelyn Cullity, and Mister McGurk.

Those friends and fellow students at Goddard College who allowed me to subject them to some truly cringe-worthy early writing and my (perhaps slightly more than) occasional madness, especially Cerridwen Elektra Aker, Mark Anderson, Corey Tacoh Bell, Jordan Bromley, Antonia Ciarovino, Josh Dean, Emily Arden Eakland, Corey Gleisberg, Jason Hecker, Rachel Aiden Holmes, Simone John, Seneca Kristjonsdottir, Christiana Wyly Musk, David Runge, Mrs. & Mr. Emma Mullington Schlenoff, Brandy Bonomo Schultz, Claire Seisfeld, Sarah Simpson, Morgan Lindsey Tachco, Liz Uzzell, and yes, even you, Reza.

Joshua Amses, whose friendship never fails to dispel that cloud of anxiety hovering above us (both) all, supplanting it (and I think you'll like this, Josh) with love and light! Of the best sort. Obviously.

Michael Dobos and Vincent Resh, who gave me family when it felt like I had none along with endless hours of counsel, critique, cig-time, fried food, huge G's cheap wine, binge-worthy television, support, and love that stays with me no matter how life changes.

The Ladies (and at least a few of the Gentlemen) of the Inn at Shelburne Farms, who, knowingly or not, helped me through the writing of this book and the darkness that often accompanied it, especially Morgan Acampora, Sarah Auger, Lindsey Carter, Jillian DeStefano, Laura Greaney, William Iliff, Emily Magarian, Miranda Mello, Meg Precourt, Sarah Raabe (and family), Zarah Savoie, Maureen Sullivan, and Sam Wisnewski.

And all those who knew me in earlier years, while I yet maintained the lie, those who, again, knowingly or not, supported me despite too often suffering the effects of my secret and the carefully constructed walls I built around it and all the lengths I went to protecting and reinforcing and denying its very presence and all the conflict that existed between. I hope this book offers something of an explanation.

Finally, my largest debt of gratitude will always and ever be held by my wife, Kathryn Roberts Bucca. Without you, Kate, I doubt that this book would ever have come to fruition. Without you, life as I now know it would only ever have been a distant, unfulfilled hope that I couldn't begin to conceptualize enough to hope for. Thank you for all you give me; your love, your trust, and your steadfast belief. Thank you for the clarity you bring to every muddy human interaction and the intelligence you lend to my understanding of an often difficult-to-understand world. Thank you for your honesty. Thank you for hearing every thought I voice and reading every word I write. Thank you for showing me what life can be and for your willingness to create that life with me. I love you, and I'm so grateful for you.

IOWA PRIZE FOR LITERARY NONFICTION

China Lake: A Journey into the Contradicted
Heart of a Global Climate Catastrophe
by Barret Baumgart

For Single Mothers Working as Train Conductors
by Laura Esther Wolfson

When You Learn the Alphabet
by Kendra Allen

Faculty Brat: A Memoir of Abuse
by Dominic Bucca